# Milford

## Sarum Studies I

# Richard Durman

Introduction                                                    3
1    Where or what is Milford?                                  5
2    The Early Days                                            12
3    Milford in 1800                                           20
4    After 1800                                                25
5    Milford Hollow and Clarendon Way                          36
6    The Railways                                              41
7    The Godolphin School                                      46
8    People                                                    52
9    All Change at Milford?                                    60
Appendices    1 Population of Milford 1801-1911                68
              2 Tithe Award 1845                               68
              3 Extract from *Wilts & Somerset Woollen Mills*  70

Bibliography                                                   70

Index                                                          72

First published in the United Kingdom in 2007, on behalf of the Sarum Chronicle Editorial Team, by
The Hobnob Press, PO Box 1838, East Knoyle, Salisbury SP3 6FA.
© Richard Durman 2007

British Library Cataloguing in Publication Data
A catalogue record for this book is available from the British Library.

ISBN 978-0-946418-60-2
Typeset in 11/13 pt Octavian.  Typesetting and origination by John Chandler
Printed in Great Britain by Salisbury Printing Company Ltd, Salisbury

# Introduction

THE STORY OF SALISBURY is well known: how the Iron Age
hill fort at Old Sarum came to be used first by the Romans, then
by the Saxons and finally by the Norman invaders, who made it both the
principal town of Wiltshire and the centre of a great diocese. All this has
been the subject of much research and historical writing. So too has the
later creation and rapid rise of the new city of Salisbury ('New Sarum')
and the building of a new cathedral. It is an exciting and important series
of events that has been extensively covered in recent times by John
Chandler in *Endless Street*, first published in 1983, and supplemented
by Ruth Newman and Jane Howells (*Salisbury Past*, 2001) and by Bruce
Purvis (*Salisbury the Changing City*, 2003). The story was brought to an
even wider audience in 1987 by the publication of Edward Rutherfurd's
'epic bestseller' *Sarum*, a novel of Salisbury and its Plain over a time span
of 'a hundred centuries'.

The main thrust of all this research and writing has been in
relation to Old and New Sarum, that is to say, the area of the hillfort and
the settlement that adjoined it, and the new medieval city laid out in grid-
like fashion (the 'Chequers') and the Cathedral Close. But the present-
day city of Salisbury embraces an area much wider than the Chequers
and, since its rapid expansion from the middle of the 19th century, has
absorbed many of the small settlements that existed long before the
creation of New Sarum. The purpose of this book is to concentrate on
one of those settlements, Milford. The ambiguities that surround the
name 'Milford' are discussed in Chapter 1, but, for most purposes,
Milford is best thought of today as Salisbury's eastern suburb, that was
first developed in a significant way in the 19th century.

The greater part of the text will relate to Victorian Milford, to the
period during which the present character of the place was formed. But
there is much of interest in Milford's earlier history. It was the Victorian
development that brought to light the first known phase of Milford's

history (or, strictly speaking, pre-history), more than 200,000 years ago, when, even while the very geology of the place was still being formed, it was being frequented by early humans. Recorded events in Milford itself are hard to come by, but it is not too difficult to extrapolate what we know about places nearby (Old Sarum, New Sarum, Clarendon Palace) to draw a few conclusions about Milford in Saxon and medieval times. The fact that the Bishop of Salisbury owned the manor of Milford has played a significant part in its story. By the 18th century, Milford, though still lightly populated, had become an attractive, and sometimes lively, spot to live in and visit, and, with a little imagination, this can still be recreated in one's mind today.

There are many people whom I wish to thank for their various contributions; some are referred to in appropriate footnotes, but special mention needs to be made of Ruth Newman who helped me to tie up some loose ends early on and later read the text and made valuable suggestions; Bruce Purvis, Salisbury reference librarian, Steve Hobbs, Wiltshire & Swindon Record Office, and Lorna Haycock, librarian of Devizes Museum, who were all unfailingly helpful in directing me to appropriate material. I also obtained valuable assistance from Peter Saunders and staff of the Salisbury & South Wiltshire Museum, from John Walsh and Stephen Lycett of The Godolphin School and Nick Stiven of Chafyn Grove School; and on palaeontology from Wessex Archaeology (especially Phil Harding); Nick Griffiths was generous with his time in connection with the Saxon period and Helena Cave-Penny supplied useful data on archaeology in Milford. Brian and Bette Barber contributed much useful material about the Barber family and on other local matters.

The following have kindly given approval for the reproduction of the illustrations indicated: Wiltshire & Swindon Record Office (pp. 20, 26, 30 top, 58); Salisbury & South Wiltshire Museum (p. 24); Irwell Press (p. 42); Brian Barber (p. 32 bottom); Edwin Young Collection, Salisbury Library (cover and pp. 38, 39, 62).

# 1
# Where or What is 'Milford'?

**W**E NEED FIRST to consider whether Milford is capable of definition and whether, in the twenty-first century, it can be said to exist. This will involve looking at early local settlements called Milford and other areas or locations to which the name has been attached.

The origin or derivation of English place-names can often present difficulties and the need to refer to a specialised dictionary. For example, it may not immediately be obvious that 'Salisbury' is 'the borough of the stronghold at *Sorvio*', or Laverstock 'the outlying farmstead or hamlet frequented by larks'. By comparison, the name 'Milford' contains no surprises – simply, 'ford by a mill'. It is a common place-name, with examples in Derbyshire, Devon, Staffordshire and Surrey as well as the slightly puzzling 'Milford on Sea' in Hampshire. Its modern spelling had become established by the 17th century but earlier versions were Meleford, Muleford, Mileford, Mulleford, Melford and Mivord.[1]

Nor is it difficult to guess the location of the ford and mill: it is almost certainly a reference to a spot on the River Bourne at or near the medieval bridge (Milford Bridge) and former mill that we can see today. However, there is no evidence of there ever having been a settlement actually by the side of the river. The more likely location is 300 metres or so to the west, around the crossroads by the side of Milford Manor.[2] The River Bourne, being a winterbourne, is not liable to regular flooding, but

1  See Gover under 'Milford'.
2  Certainly this is where it is shown in a useful map entitled 'Roads, settlements etc. before 1220' published in 1980 by the Royal Commission on Historic Monuments (England) as part of their report on the *Ancient and Historical Monuments in the City of Salisbury (Volume 1)*.

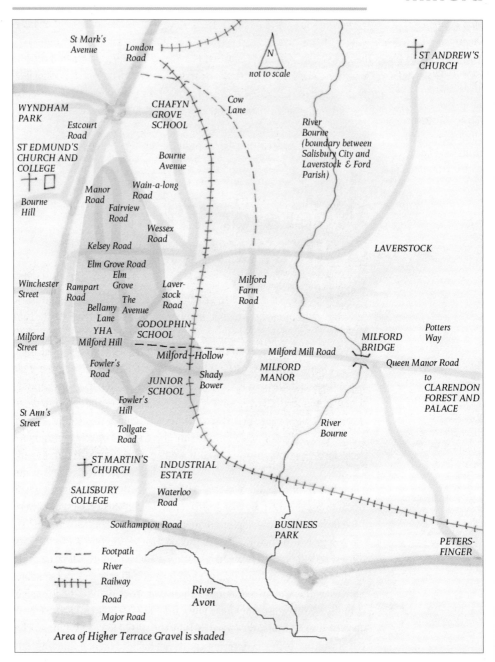

St Mark's Avenue

London Road

N
not to scale

†ST ANDREW'S CHURCH

WYNDHAM PARK

Estcourt Road

CHAFYN GROVE SCHOOL

Cow Lane

River Bourne (boundary between Salisbury City and Laverstock & Ford Parish)

ST EDMUND'S CHURCH AND COLLEGE

Bourne Avenue

Bourne Hill

Manor Road

Wain-a-long Road

Fairview Road

Wessex Road

Kelsey Road

LAVERSTOCK

Elm Grove Road

Elm Grove

Winchester Street

Rampart Road

The Avenue

Laverstock Road

Milford Farm Road

Bellamy Lane

Milford Street

YHA Milford Hill

GODOLPHIN SCHOOL

Potters Way

MILFORD BRIDGE

Fowler's Road

Milford Hollow

Milford Mill Road

MILFORD MANOR

Queen Manor Road

to CLARENDON FOREST AND PALACE

JUNIOR SCHOOL

Shady Bower

Fowler's Hill

St Ann's Street

Tollgate Road

River Bourne

†ST MARTIN'S CHURCH

INDUSTRIAL ESTATE

SALISBURY COLLEGE

Waterloo Road

Southampton Road

BUSINESS PARK

PETERS-FINGER

– – – – Footpath

River

+++++ Railway

Road

Major Road

River Avon

Area of Higher Terrace Gravel is shaded

it does occasionally overflow its banks, and it is obviously more prudent to build on ground at the edge of, or beyond, the natural floodplain. The settlement on this side of the river was 'Milford Episcopi' (Bishop's Milford), but there were once two other settlements, or, strictly speaking, estates, containing the name Milford on the other side of the river, namely

*Map 1, [opposite] Diagrammatic map of principal features of present-day Milford. Also shown shaded is the area of Higher Terrace Gravel in which Stone Age axe heads have been found in abundance.*

Milford Pichard and Milford Richard.[3] There is no evidence of exactly where they were sited but it is unlikely that they lay far from the river, because in 1386 it was recorded that the bridge at that time had been repaired 'time out of mind' by all three settlements. Indeed, it is probable that at least one of them lay nearer to the river than Milford Episcopi since the ground rises up from the river (and therefore away from the floodplain) more quickly on the east side than on the west. Archaeology has begun to reveal the full extent of the Laverstock pottery industry east of the Bourne (see Chapter 2) but more excavations will be required if the settlement pattern is to be better understood.

*Milford Bridge (14th century) – probably on, or close to the site of the original ford across the River Bourne and a replacement of an earlier Saxon bridge.*

In Volume 6 of the *Victoria History of Wiltshire* the assumption is made that 1386 was the year in which the existing Milford Bridge was constructed, replacing an earlier structure. In view of the importance of the east–west route across the river in Saxon times it is very likely that the first bridge was built (perhaps in timber) before the Norman Conquest.[4]

Although the area containing all three settlements, which we can tentatively call 'Milford', straddled the River Bourne, the river also divided it in significant ways. The first is that the land to the west was

3   In a calendar of Feet of Fines for Wiltshire in the reign of Elizabeth I, they are rendered as 'Milford Pynchard' and 'Ilford [*sic*] Rychard'.

4   David Harrison in an article 'Medieval Bridges' in *History Today* Vol. 54 (11) November 2004 explains that the bulk of the pre-industrial bridge network was built between 750 and 1250; that Anglo-Saxon bridges were constructed with timber roadways resting on timber or stone piers.

the bishop's and the land to the east was the king's. It was in 1075, in accordance with a decree of the Council of London requiring cathedrals to be sited in more populous and better defended places than in Saxon times, that Herman, the Bishop of Sherborne and Ramsbury, 'carried his stool' to Old Sarum as the first Bishop of Salisbury. The new diocese comprised Wiltshire, Dorset and Berkshire. It was probably in the early part of the 12th century that a bishop's manor was created, out of a larger tract of land belonging to the bishop. This extended southwards from Old Sarum and Stratford and was enclosed on the west and south by the River Avon and on the east by the River Bourne. The manor lay wholly within the ancient parish of St Martin, but by 1275 (the first recorded instance) the manor was being referred to as the manor of Milford. When the city of New Sarum came to be created from

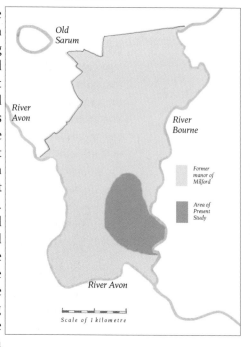

Map 2. The Manor of Milford, belonging to the Bishop of Salisbury, as it was before the creation of New Sarum, with the area of the present study superimposed.

about 1200 the land for it would therefore have been carved from the south-western corner of the bishop's manor. Once the city's boundaries were established, the city comprised its own 'city' manor, with the bishop as its lord, and the rest of the larger manor became known as Milford.

This explains why there is an 18th-century house (now a hotel) called Milford Hall in Castle Street, lying not far from the River Avon (where it forms the western boundary of the medieval city) and just outside the original northern limits of the city. It also explains why, in the 19th century, a census area called Milford embraced the properties to the north of the medieval chequers. But, most significantly of all, the manor did not include any land to the east of the River Bourne. For this was, and had long been, the royal demesne of Clarendon, favoured and enhanced by the Plantagenet kings, but possibly first established as a royal hunting park in Saxon times.[5] One of the royal possessions was the mill at Milford: it was never recorded as belonging to the bishop, and a 'water-mill' at Milford 'held of the King in chief' is mentioned more than

---

5    One piece of evidence for this is the ring bearing the name of Æthelwulf (King of Wessex 839-58, father of Alfred) found in the late 18th century in Laverstock, that is to say on the king's land on the east side of the river. It is unlikely that the wearer of the ring had been Æthelwulf himself but could well have been someone close to him and to whom the ring had been given.

once in medieval property inquisitions.[6] Although the *manor* of Milford stopped short of the Bourne, the name had been attached to settlements on the king's side, Milford Pichard and Milford Richard. It seems absurd that two adjoining settlements should have such similar names, but Pichard was possibly pronounced 'Peyechard', rather than rhyming with Richard, reducing the risk of confusion in an age when communication was largely oral. The name 'Richard' appears to have been derived from the fact that in the first half of the 13th century one of the three foresters of Clarendon Forest was Richard of Milford who held land and property, including a water mill, in Milford directly from the king.[7] This part of Milford, presumably close to the Bourne, may (for whatever reason) have become so closely associated with him that the name stuck.

The other significant split of Milford was between 'hundreds', the territorial areas created in Saxon times into which a county was divided. They were used for taxation purposes throughout the Middle Ages, and in connection with population censuses until 1881, and a divided Milford was always an anomaly. To the west of the Bourne lay the hundred of Underditch; to the east lay the hundred of Alderbury.[8] The split was reflected in the records that have survived for taxation purposes. The tax roll of 1334, which largely reflects those of 1269, 1297, 1327 and 1332,[9] contains an entry for Milford in both hundreds. The taxable value of the movables on which tax was levied was put at 78 shillings in respect of people living in Underditch and at 20 shillings in respect of those in Alderbury. We can only guess at what Milford amounted to in each case but it may be that the 'Alderbury' Milford comprised Pichard and Richard but that the 'Underditch' Milford comprised, not only the small settlement at Episcopi, but the entire bishop's manor. Both Salisbury and Old Sarum were separately assessed. The discrepancy between the two Milfords is even greater in the lists of poll-tax payers of 1377 with 119 in Underditch and only 20 in Alderbury.

Adding to the confusion is the fact that Milford has never had its own parish church; this prevented it, or any part of it, from being treated as a parish until 1881, when it became a civil parish. Before then the entire

6　See e.g. Wiltshire Inquisitions Henry III and Edward III held at Devizes Museum.

7　VCH vol.4 p.430.

8　Underditch also contained the 'vills' of Heale, Lake, Stratford-sub-Castle, Wilsford and Great and Little Woodford. By 1831 the *parishes* that made up Underditch were Stratford-sub-Castle, Wilsford, Woodford and part of Laverstock and Ford (i.e. part Milford and part Ford). Alderbury Hundred extended to the village of that name and beyond.

9　See VCH vol.4 pp. 294-302.

area of Milford (west and east of the Bourne) was treated as a 'tithing', a unit for church taxation purposes – at first (until 1841) of the ancient parish of Laverstock and Ford (even though the parish itself did not extend west of the Bourne) and later (from 1841 to 1881) of Salisbury St Martin. Parishes and hundreds were the areas used for population censuses from 1801 onwards and the anomalous position of Milford was again highlighted, but not resolved. Volume 4 of the *Victoria History of Wiltshire* contains a valuable table of population figures for censuses in the county between 1801 and 1951. In the case of other places that have been absorbed by Salisbury as it extended its boundaries – Fisherton Anger, West Harnham and Stratford-sub-Castle – it is a simple matter to read off the population figures for each 10-year census until that place disappears into the city. This cannot be done for Milford because it appears in no less than six different entries in the table. A digest of the details is contained in Appendix 1.

In 1835 the city boundaries were extended eastwards as far as the top of Milford Hill,[10] but it seems this did not affect the boundaries of Milford, at any rate for the purpose of tithe commutation – the exercise that would soon be underway across the country for converting (or 'commuting') the payment of tithes into the payment of fixed sums of money (rentcharges).

The Tithe Apportionment and Map for Milford produced in 1845 treats the land within the tithing as wrapping round the Chequers and extending northwards to the Roman road at Ford, westwards roughly to the line of Castle Road, southwards to the River Avon and eastwards to the River Bourne. But, unlike the manor of the same name, it also extended beyond the Bourne to include fields and properties (south of Queen Manor Road) along both sides of Petersfinger Road as far as the junction with Southampton Road. This document is particularly valuable for giving us a snapshot of Milford at a critical moment in its history, just before the coming of the railway, the arrival of The Godolphin School and, most importantly, the onset of suburban development. Appendix 2 contains a breakdown of the land in the tithing at that time, together with some details of the awards and of a few of the properties.

In 1894 the part of Milford that had been incorporated within Salisbury was constituted the parish of Milford Within, and the part lying

---

10  i.e. the street of that name. The term Milford Hill has come to mean either of two things: the hill to the east of the medieval city that became an important magnet for suburban development in the 19th century; or the street that leads from the east end of Milford Street to the top of the hill called Milford Hill! (A more logical name, perhaps, would have been Milford Hill Road.) The sense in which the term is being used hereafter will, I trust, be clear from its context.

outside the city, including land on the east side of the River Bourne, was constituted the parish of Milford Without.

In 1904 the city boundaries were extended once again, this time as far as the River Bourne. The part of Milford Without that lay west of the river became absorbed within Salisbury, and that to the east within the parish of Laverstock. This was not quite the end of Milford however. At the same time, a new parish of Milford was created from part of Milford Without and part of Ford. But in 1905 this parish merged with Salisbury and, in a formal sense at least, Milford finally ceased to exist. Its former existence and identity lives on as a name attached to many things – a number of streets, a hill, a bridge, a former manor house, a farm, a nursing home, a hotel, a former railway station and, above all an area of Salisbury, albeit vague and undefined, still referred to as Milford. For many years it was also the name of a ward of the District of Salisbury lying wholly within the city, although in 1999 the Milford Ward was split between St Edmund Ward and St Martin Ward, giving us today a St Edmund and Milford Ward and a St Martin and Milford Ward. Not that, even before 1999, could Milford Ward necessarily be equated with a true place called Milford. District Wards need to be given some sort of a name to distinguish one from another; 'Milford' may have been regarded as an appropriate name for the ward because it broadly corresponded with that part of Salisbury traditionally known as Milford, but that does not mean that its boundaries were those of Milford.

Reference should also be made to the Milford Preservation Group, established in 1980 'to take action when appropriate to preserve the character and amenities of the Milford area for the benefit of householders in the area'. 'The Milford area' for this purpose comprises an area consisting of the southern end of Milford Hill extending eastwards to include that part of Laverstock traditionally regarded as being part of Milford, as far as Potters Way and the Petersfinger area.

For the purposes of this present study, Milford will comprise the whole of Milford Hill (as far northwards as the end of Manor Road ('Weeping Cross') and the old settlement of Milford Episcopi, as far eastwards as Milford Bridge. It will not venture into Laverstock except to mention the settlements there that once contained the name Milford. So, unless the context requires another meaning, this is what 'Milford' will mean throughout the following chapters.

# 2
# The Early Days

**M**ANY LOCAL HISTORIES of places in England begin with Domesday Book of 1086. Some are able to refer to an earlier Saxon or Roman presence or to evidence of even earlier occupation in the Iron Age, going back to, say, 500 BC. In Wiltshire, the county of Stonehenge and Avebury, it is not unusual to be able to lay claim to sites that go back a further 4,000 years – the causewayed enclosures, henges, long barrows and other monuments of the Bronze Age or New Stone Age. None of these exist at Milford and whilst one or more of its three early settlements (Episcopi, Pichard and Richard) may well have had Saxon origins, there is nothing on the ground to show for it. Indeed, its oldest monument is Milford Bridge from the 14th century. And yet it contains one of those rare sites in Britain that have been found to contain evidence of human presence ('occupation' would be too strong a word) at a time so long ago that it is almost impossible to imagine. The site is on and around Milford Hill and the artefacts discovered there date from about 200,000 to 250,000 years ago. More will be said about them and the circumstances of their discovery in Chapter 4.

Until very recently, palaeontologists believed that the first humans had reached Britain from Africa about 500,000 years ago, though, following discoveries in Clacton in 2005, that stage has been put back to 700,000 years ago. This was not *Homo sapiens*, who did not come to Britain until about 40-50,000 years ago, but is more likely to have been *Homo heidelbergensis*, an earlier link in the long chain between early primates and modern man. To all intents and purposes the builders of Stonehenge and Avebury can be regarded as having the same innate physical and mental attributes as ourselves. The people roaming southern England a quarter of a million years ago, perhaps only numbering 2,000, would be much closer to the popular image of 'Stone Age Man', the hairy

*An example of the 309 early Stone Age axes found on Milford Hill by Dr H. Blackmore and Mr E. T. Stevens while development was taking place there in the 19th century. They were evidence that the Hill was an important site to early humans about 250,000 years ago (drawing reduced to approximately half actual size).*

hunter-gatherer concerned with little more than the next meal. Yet if that meal were to contain meat it was dependent on highly-developed skills in making flint axe heads and cutting tools. And, within the river organization of the Avon,[11] Milford Hill was one of the two most important sites (the other being Woodgreen to the south) to which these early people came to make those tools. River levels here were 20-30m higher than today and Milford Hill stood at the confluence of two wide rivers. This was all so long ago that it is going back into geological time when the very land of Britain was still being formed. Within the Avon system, beds of flinty gravel were still being laid down where rivers bent or joined. This has had at least two effects on Salisbury's history: the attraction of Milford Hill to these early bands of nomads and the presence of the bed of gravel on which the cathedral was built, ensuring its long-term stability.

11   That is to say the area drained by the Avon and its various tributaries, the most important being the Rivers Nadder, Wylye, Bourne and Ebble.

After these exceptional beginnings, people do not appear to have left their mark on Milford again until relatively recent times. One might expect land on either side of the River Bourne, close to the main artery of the Avon and to the important ritual landscape around Stonehenge, to start to be inhabited from, say, 3,000 years ago. Yet, whilst there is evidence of prehistoric occupation and use of the higher ground to the east of Laverstock and at Bishopsdown (to give it its proper name), none has come to light in respect of Milford Hill. Nor has any Romano-British use of the area been detected. Indeed, the next recorded find is 'Anglo-Saxon', namely a skeleton found in 1878 'on the east side of a road across Mr E. Kelsey's Milford Hill Building Estate'. The skeleton's head pointed to the north-west and its feet to the south-east, and had been buried with an iron spearhead, a small knife and an iron chisel.

This find lends support to the possibility that one or more of the Milford settlements were of Saxon origin. As indeed do more extensive finds on the other side of the Bourne at Milford Farm and on the line of the railway west of Petersfinger. The first was a fragment of pottery thought to date from the 5th to 7th centuries. Although it was found within the area occupied in connection with the well-known medieval Laverstock pottery industry, it is unlikely to be evidence of a Saxon pre-cursor of that industry, merely of Saxon presence. The Petersfinger finds were burials and associated goods, thought to date from the 5th and 6th centuries. This cemetery is one of four such sites in the Salisbury area that were probably associated with settlements close to Old Sarum, the local principal place both as the Roman *Sorviodunum* (when it was a nodal point of the Roman road system) and later as the Saxon *Searobryg*. The other sites, all close to the Avon or Bourne, are at Winterbourne Gunner, Harnham and Charlton. This is a part of Wessex in which there appears to have been a foreign presence (Germanic and/or Frankish) even while the British were still the dominant population. In the century and a half after Britain was left by Rome to fend for itself (in 410) the presence of Saxons in the area may at first have been a source of mild concern before later becoming a serious threat. Local Saxon domination would come in 552 after the defeat of the British at Old Sarum by the Saxon king Cynric.

It is likely that the Petersfinger cemetery was associated with Mumworth, the lost settlement at the confluence of the Bourne and Avon, rather than Milford Richard or Milford Pichard, which are more likely to have come into existence after the Norman Conquest. Milford Episcopi, or at any rate some kind of settlement west of the Bourne, may already have been in existence. For 'lands which in Domesday the bishop is said to have been held in demesne [i.e. for his own use], and was cultivated by means of servile tenants, were partly on Milford hill.'[12] The bishop's villeinage lay 'beyond the barrier or gate leading to St Martin's church.'[13] Domesday Book, compiled for William I in 1086, also refers to two pieces of land at 'Milford' each of 'half a hide' (a hide was usually between 60 and 120 acres) and in each case half of the land lay within the king's forest. This seems to mean, firstly, that the River Bourne flowed through the middle of each holding and, secondly, that the name Milford was being applied to the area in the vicinity of the river crossing and mill rather than to a nucleated settlement. On the other hand, a reason for believing that one came to exist, at least by the early 13th century, is the line of the route (of which more will be said in Chapter 5) between Winchester, the capital of Wessex, and Wilton, the chief town in Wiltshire. This came past Clarendon Palace, across the ford (or, later, the bridge) at Milford and thence westwards to Fisherton Bridge. The medieval route from Amesbury to Alderbury also used this crossing of the Bourne at Milford. There are two examples nearby, namely Fisherton and East Harnham, of early settlements that grew up on a well-established route close to where it crossed a river and it is likely that the same occurred at Milford.

In time, this settlement would be Milford Episcopi but, on the other side of the Bourne, within a part of Laverstock then known as Milford,[14] was the site of the important medieval pottery industry, now always referred to as the 'Laverstock' industry. It flourished during the 13th and 14th centuries and was probably established in the 12th. Nine kilns were found between 1958 and 1963 in allotment gardens north of Queen Manor Road and west of Duck Lane. The site, now Potters Way, was being developed for housing by Mr E. Fielden, who presented all the pottery that was found, over 40 sackfuls of it, to the Salisbury & South Wilts Museum, where much of it is on display. As we have seen, this was on the king's side of the Bourne and the industry was probably established to meet the needs of Clarendon Palace, but its products later reached Salisbury and beyond. Apart from pots, the potters manufactured a range of products used in building, such as ridge and corner tiles, drainpipes, chimney pots, louvres and floor tiles. The industry appears to have declined after the 14th century in line with a lessening in royal interest in Clarendon Palace. The lost settlements of Milford Richard and Milford Pichard may have grown out of the Laverstock pottery industry and

12  Benson and Hatcher p.42.

13  ibid.

14  A record of 1270 speaks of an allocation to the sheriff of Wiltshire of 25s for 1000 pitchers bought and carried from Muleford (Milford ) [see Musty et al.].

declined with it. Pottery finds on Milford Farm, south of Queen Manor Road, indicate that the full extent of the kiln area may not yet have been found. If or when further excavations take place more light may be thrown too on the medieval settlement pattern east of the Bourne.

By the beginning of the 13th century, Milford was one of the places close to the site of New Sarum that would be referred to confusingly as the 'Old Salisburies'. The others were the little settlement around the bishop's mill on the Avon, which became absorbed within the new city, and the more substantial St Martin, which remained outside the city limits but hard up against them. Milford retained a more distinctive identity, being rather more removed from New Sarum. However, little light can be shed on what medieval life there may have been like. Its character was clearly rural and, in part, cultivated; but in the words of the *Victoria History of Wiltshire* 'little is known of the agrarian organisation of Milford in the Middle Ages'. It goes on to cite a number of relevant records in relation to 'Milford', but these appear to relate to Bishopsdown and Bugmore, both within the bishop's manor, or to the part now in Laverstock. In the late 14th century it is recorded that there were 25 virgates within the manor of Milford for which was paid 'by ancient custom' 2s 6d a virgate (a measure of land usually amounting to 30 acres). But these could have been anywhere in the rural area south of Old Sarum and between the rivers. A fulling mill, probably on the site of the present Milford Mill, is recorded at Milford in 1390 and was in use until 1558. (A woollen mill here is referred to again in the next Chapter.)

The rebuilding of the bridge in the 14th century would have been an important local event. Its site was well chosen. Two branches of the river join at this point and the middle section of the bridge rests, in effect, on an island. It is likely that the procedure for its construction would have been to divert the flow of water from one branch to the other, first away from one side of the island and then from the other, enabling each half of the bridge to be built on dry land, while the water flowed by on the other side of the island. If the bridge had been built further upstream, where the two branches of the river are further apart, the structure would have had to have been a good deal longer; if downstream, where the river is wider, some sort of artificial island might have had to be created first. It is thought that Ayleswade (or Harnham) Bridge was built on these lines more than a hundred years earlier, with the creation of an artificial island that still exists.

By the standards of the time, life for the residents of Milford Episcopi may have been more favoured than in many other places in England, especially after the creation of the new city on the far side of the hill. The city itself, barely a mile away, provided a ready market for commodities of every description, and the cathedral would have been a source of wonder and inspiration for all but the dullest. As the city grew and became more crowded and polluted, the men and women of Milford would have been only too happy to return to their rural dwellings near the Bourne, however humble and crude those dwellings may have been. Their children would have been excited by the bustle of the city, especially on the days of the Tuesday and Saturday markets and during the October fair. Perhaps it fuelled their ambitions to engage in one of the many trades that they saw being practised, and become part of this more exciting urban way of life.

It may also have been an advantage to have a bishop as one's lord. The burghers of Salisbury also had the bishop as their Lord of the City and regularly chafed at what they perceived to be excessive control and interference. And yet, as Chandler has argued convincingly, the citizens most probably benefited from the exercise by successive bishops of the power and authority that came from their ownership of the city; 'by all accounts they were good landlords and just rulers, their demand for rents and taxes were reasonable and their administration was acceptably efficient.'[15]

The broad structure of this rural existence would have prevailed until the early part of the 19th century when the effects of the Industrial Revolution and a rapid increase in population began to affect people's lives in all but the remotest parts of England. This is not to say, of course, that a place like Milford would have been untouched by social change stemming from major national events, most notably the Black Death in the 14th century, the upheavals in the 16th century caused by Henry VIII's divorce from Catharine of Aragon, and, in the following century, the Civil War.

Locally, the authority of the bishop began a gradual decline after the creation of the Anglican Church. Until 1549 the bishop had from time to time granted leases of parts of the manor of Milford, but general control remained in his hands. This was to change forever in that year when the first lease of the entire manor (though with Bishopsdown Farm reserved) was granted for 99 years to William Herbert, soon to become the 1st Earl of Pembroke. There would follow a series of long leases until, in the 19th century, the land became, by Act of Parliament, part of the estates of the Ecclesiastical Commissioners. In the city, the bishop's authority had already begun to wane in favour of the municipal authorities, and in 1612 Salisbury received its first 'independent' charter.

15  *Endless Street* p. 161.

Bishopsdown Farm consisted of about 480 acres and lay in the northern part of Milford manor. The other 700 acres or so within the manor consisted in 1650 (when there was a Parliamentary survey) of five leasehold and fourteen copyhold tenements. The largest holding was called Milford Farm (not to be confused with the present Milford Farm on the east side of the River Bourne). Its size and location changed from time to time but included land on each side of London Road as well as the area to the south around the old settlement of Milford Episcopi. By the 19th century it was farmed in two parts – 82 acres in the north, from the house now called Little Manor and the farm buildings that lay to the north of it, and 32 acres in the south from Milford Manor and its farm buildings. Bishopsdown Farm continued to be dealt with separately from the rest during the 16th and 17th centuries but early in the 18th century was included in the lease of the whole manor.

However, during the 18th century there was an attempt by its tenant Mr Henchman to have 'Bishop's Down Manor' acknowledged by the bishop as separated from Milford Manor. He cited a number of documents as evidence of that separation, adding that the reason he could not cite more was that 'those deeds were burnt in Mr Gauntlett's house

*Little Manor (late 17th century), Milford's oldest surviving house, now much extended and used as a nursing home; it was built as a farmhouse, later being used (probably) as an inn, a rectory and a private dwelling.*

at Netherhampton who was then Steward of the Pembroke family'.[16] Henchman, in other words, was trying to achieve legal parity with the lessee for the time being of Milford manor, a parity that would, for example, allow him to retain rent and other payments in relation to Bishopsdown instead of their going to the lessee of Milford manor. In his letter to the bishop he argued that there would be no danger of exercising his rights irresponsibly since he was 'too much under the Eye of the Bishop of Sarum'. However, he clearly did not succeed because, as we enter the next century, the manor of Milford remained under a single lease. It still comprised all the land between the rivers Avon and Bourne below a line roughly south of the Roman road from Ford to Old Sarum, except that the Chequers were excluded as was most of the land between Castle Road and the River Avon.[17]

*A section of the 300-year-old wall of Milford Manor in Milford Mill Road.*

16  Letter ('18th cent.') WSRO ref CC158/4.
17  Map of Milford Estate of William Beckford [WSRO ref CC27]; Map of the Manor of Milford [WSRO ref CC45/357].

# 3
# Milford in 1800

**B**Y 1800 the leaseholder of the manor was one of the wealthiest and best-known figures of late-Georgian England, William Beckford, of whom there will be more in Chapter 8. A lease of the manors of Milford and Woodford had been granted to his father, William ('Alderman') Beckford in 1764; on his death in 1770 it vested in the

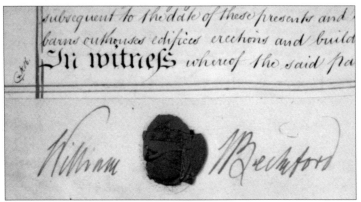

*Seal and signature of William Beckford (Lord Farmer of Milford) on a lease of land at Milford to J. G. Coombes dated 19th June 1838 (WSRO ref. Bishoprick 171/5).*

younger Beckford to whom it was renewed in 1782 and again in 1832. In documentation he is described as the Lord Farmer of Milford, a curious expression since the peerage to which he aspired was dashed from his lips by scandal and he never engaged in farming in the agricultural sense.[18] We can be certain that neither the bishop nor Beckford would ever have lived at the manor house, the predecessor of the present-day

18   The explanation is that 'farmer' is being used here of a person to whom land has been 'farmed out' for payment, deriving from the Latin *firma*, a fixed fee; and 'Lord' since the leaseholder would have been entitled to many rights of the lordship though not himself Lord of the Manor, who remained the bishop.

Milford Manor at the bottom of Shady Bower. Indeed, it is doubtful if there was ever a true manor house at Milford. The oldest house recorded as a 'manor house' on the site was built in the late 17th or 18th century, and served as a farmhouse during the 18th and 19th centuries. An estate map of 1778 shows a small farmyard and farm buildings on the outside of the bend of what is now Shady Bower, close to but separate from the manor house. There are two survivals of the old house – a length of old wall along the south side of Milford Mill Road and a summerhouse. The wall was partly re-built in about 2000. The summerhouse now lies within the garden of one of the houses in Milford Manor Gardens laid out in 1986. There is also another structure just inside Milford Manor Gardens, sometimes rather fancifully called 'The Orangery'; this is made up from recycled stone and other materials from the former house.

This former manor house may well simply have been the latest in a series of houses on this central site. There were three other substantial buildings in Milford in 1800 that were likely to have replaced earlier structures. Two are the 18th-century houses now known as 'Mill House' and 'The Granary' straddling the River Bourne, with a small millwheel house between them, just to the north of Milford Bridge. In a map of 1773 the legend 'Tocking mill' appears against them, indicating the continued existence of the Salisbury woollen trade – since tucking was the local term for fulling. The woollen mills of Wiltshire and Somerset were the subject of research published in 1976; the item concerning Milford is set out in full in Appendix 3. There is no evidence of there being a corn mill here. However, the map also shows a waterway running parallel to the main river that crossed Milford Mill Road a little way to the west and ran along the edge of the grounds of the manor house before rejoining the Bourne. It is possible that it had been cut to provide power to another mill in this locality.

The other 'new' building on a site that had probably been used before is 'Little Manor' (as it is now called) built in the later part of the 17th century. It has had a chequered career. Its first use was as a residence associated with the farm buildings to the north. (These existed until about 1972 when, along with a cottage facing Milford Hollow, they were demolished prior to the development of the site for housing in Milford Manor Road and Westbourne Close). At some stage it may have been an inn, the 'Travellers' Rest'.[19] When the new church at Laverstock was

---

19  Haskins says of 'The Travellers' Rest', Milford: 'This is said to have been the house which at present is the residence of the vicar of Laverstock.' (Haskins lived at No. 7 Wain-a-long Road and was presiding alderman for Milford Ward)

built (*c*. 1858) it became the rectory. It was not until a new purpose-built rectory was built in Laverstock in 1934 that it became a private house and, for the first time, was called 'Little Manor'. It stands at the east end of Milford Hollow; on the opposite side were the stables serving the manor house.

*Brome House, Milford Hollow, now part of The Godolphin School and enclosed within its grounds. The oldest section (with entrance porch) was once the 'Blue Post' inn.*

The 1773 map shows a good sprinkling of other buildings along both Milford Hollow and Shady Bower. Shady Bower (not so called until 1881)[20] has a well-established look to it in the map and may have come into existence a century or two before (see Chapter 5). Two more of the buildings shown on the map had, by 1800, been granted licences as inns, making three altogether in an area that today contains a much greater population but no licensed premises![21] One was the 'Blue Post' in Milford Hollow, first licensed in 1775. The building can still be seen today within the site of The Godolphin School as the central portion of 'Brome House', having been greatly extended on both sides and to the rear in Victorian times. The other was the 'Punch Bowl' in Shady Bower that was first licensed in 1710 and occupied the present site of the blocks of flats that make up Shady Bower Close. The building itself lay towards the eastern

20  In a map of about 1850 it is still being referred to as 'drove way to Milford etc' [WSRO ref CC32]. It is called Shady Bower in the district description of the 1881 census (RG11/2070 fol.53).

21  It would be tempting to assume that this was largely due to the fact that from 1860 the manor became vested in the Ecclesiastical Commissioners (see next chapter) but the principal relevant deeds do not contain any restrictive covenants.

end of the large grounds that it occupied. This space would have been useful in August 1784 when, according to a report in the *Salisbury and Winchester Journal*[22] a pilotless Montgolfier air balloon, or a 'Grand Aerostatic Globe' fifteen feet in circumference was launched at the 'Punch Bowl', Milford. Admittance was one shilling to see the 'infusion of flammable air' and 'to the satisfaction of a very large number of spectators the balloon continued visible nearly 8 minutes . . . and was at length lost in the clouds.' Its destination was Winchester but it was found in Farley Woods, eight miles from Salisbury. From there, apparently, it was taken surreptitiously to Winchester 'where a live cat was affixed to it and good market made of the credulity of the public, by showing it and the animal as having made an aerial voyage together.' The first hot air balloon had been flown less than a year earlier in front of Louis XVI and Marie Antoinette with a sheep, a duck and a cockerel on board.

An event such as this, and the presence of three inns in such a small area surrounded by open countryside, encourages the notion that this part of Milford then served as a pleasant spot for entertainment and leisure, out of sight of Salisbury but only a short trip away, whether by carriage or on foot. A walk to Milford from the city centre would have been a drinker's paradise. Milford Street itself contained four inns, the 'Red Lion and Cross Keys' (first licensed in 1756); the 'Goat' (1736); the 'Rainbow' (1767) and the 'Cart Wheel' (1759) as well as six alehouses, the 'White Horse' (1739), the 'Three Cranes' (1734), the 'Queen's Head' (1740), the 'Noah's Ark' (1735), the 'Angel' (1732) and the 'Bell' (1774).[23] On entering Milford Hill one would soon reach on the left ('near Mrs Pinckney's Lodge')[24] the 'Weavers' Arms' alehouse for final fortification before climbing to the other establishments in Milford mentioned earlier.

It would be useful to have contemporary images of Milford, of its landscape or its buildings. Only one has come to light – a picture, painted towards the end of the 18th century, in the collection of the Salisbury & South Wilts Museum, showing Milford Bridge from the east with the River Bourne in the foreground and the cathedral in the background. It shows one or two indeterminate buildings set amongst trees and the spire of St Martin's church, but it cannot be taken as an accurate portrayal since the river appears excessively wide and far more of the cathedral is shown than can actually be seen from the east bank of the river. But the oddest thing about it is its title, *Arnon Bridge*. There can be only one plausible explanation for this. The artist had a French name and was presumably

22  Drawn to my attention by Ruth Newman.

23  These derive from Haskins, who warns that some alehouses may appear under more than one name, the tenant having changed the name.

24  As Haskins describes it in 1912.

a visitor to Salisbury. On returning to his hotel or lodging he would have been asked what he had done that day. After explaining that he had painted a picture of an old stone bridge with the cathedral in the background he would have been told, in the local accent, (and very understandably) that he 'must a bin at 'arnham bridge.' 'Arnon Bridge?' 'Thaat's roit. 'arnham Bridge.' And so *Arnon Bridge* it was.

*'Arnon Bridge' by Henri de Cort (c.1795): despite its curious name the painting clearly depicts a view across the River Bourne showing Milford Bridge, the spire of St Martin's church and (in an exaggerated form) Salisbury cathedral.*

# 4
# After 1800

UNTIL ABOUT 1800 the only part of Milford with any concentration of buildings was around the crossroads at the old Milford Episcopi and on each side of Milford Hollow and Shady Bower. This pattern would change drastically as the 19th century progressed until only two large areas remained free from new development. One was the eastern slopes of Milford Hill lying north of the old village – by World War II (WWII) they too would be entirely covered with houses, with the exception of the playing fields of The Godolphin School[25] and Chafyn Grove School. The other was the site on the south side of Shady Bower that in 1952 would become St Martin's junior school.

But the process was slow at first and not at all typical of what would follow later. Indeed, by 1840 there were only two new houses on the 'town' side of the hill. The first had been built for Dr Richard Fowler on a site that lay to the west of the road now called Fowler's Hill (or Fowlers Hill, depending on which nameplate you read). It was certainly built before 1833 (the first time it appears on a map of Salisbury) and perhaps before 1822, since a directory of Wiltshire of that year refers to Fowler as 'of Milford-hill'. The house was demolished in about 1960 and no images of it have come to light. It was followed (again, on the evidence of maps) between 1833 and 1840 by Milford Hill House (now the Youth Hostel), this time north of Milford Hill (i.e. the street of that name). Both were

25  According to Gertrude Edwards, Old Godolphin 1890-1905, it was Lord Nelson, chairman of the Governors, who 'took the Ecclesiastical Commissioners by storm when the fate of the playing fields was at stake, and what is now the playing fields stood a chance of being rows of red villas'. In *Cat O'Mary* by Dorothy L.Sayers (see Chapter 7) reference is made to playing fields 'recently acquired' to accommodate the growing numbers of pupils.

set within extensive grounds in a style that was not possible within the densely-developed chequers, and would have been seen as emulating the houses of the Close or St Edmund's College in Bourne Hill, which was still then in the occupation of the Wyndham family. Most of the grounds of Dr Fowler's house were themselves built over in the 1880s to create Fowler's Road and Fowler's Hill, and, after the house itself had been demolished (in about 1965), its site, a mere fraction of its original size, was used for 23 dwellings. Milford Hill House, on the other hand, still exists within spacious grounds.

The suburbanisation of the hill began in earnest in 1864 when the Elm Grove estate was laid out on land sold off by the Ecclesiastical Commissioners. One of the purposes for which the Commission had been created in 1836 was to take over assets held for the support of dioceses and cathedrals. Thus the bishop's freehold interest in the manor of Milford would have vested in them from that time but the lease to a Lord Farmer would have continued. However, in 1860 the Commissioners had acquired (by surrender) the leasehold interest, which was then vested in the trustees of the will of William Beckford's son-in-law Alexander, Duke of Hamilton, and the manor of Milford thereupon ceased to exist. Elm Grove estate lay to the north of the present main building of The Godolphin School and broadly comprised The Avenue, Elm Grove, Elm

*Map 3: The southern part of the 1845 Tithe Map, showing Milford as it was before the surge of building in mid to late 19th century.*

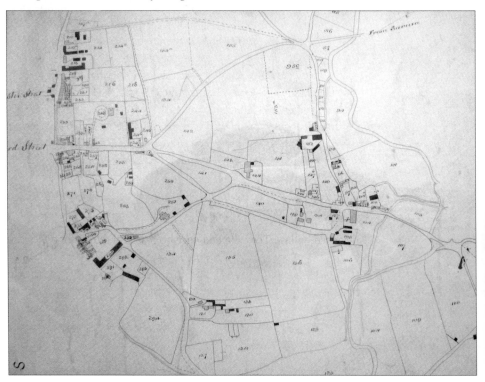

*'Manor House', Manor Road – one of the many villas being built in the expanding suburb of Milford for people wishing to move away from the centre of Salisbury.*

Grove Road, Clarendon Road and the south side of Kelsey Road. It consisted mainly of large semi-detached houses. This was followed by development of Dr Fowler's land (see above) and the laying out of Manor Road and Fairview Road as well as a tide of new houses slowly creeping up from the north side of Kelsey Road. Now we begin to see substantial detached 'villas'. The villa had once been a rural retreat for a wealthy landowner or man of affairs, a second home in the country, but from early in the 19th century the term came to be applied to almost any suburban middle-class home. As national prosperity grew in Victorian times, the businessman was no longer willing to live close to his business in town but aspired to retreat at night to his own family home beyond the edge of the town. He would either build his own villa on a plot of land that became available or buy one ready-built by a speculative builder.

In the days before a formal system of town planning existed, all this was entirely a matter of land availability and supply and demand. However, the way Milford Hill was developed from 1865 appears to have been reasonably steady and orderly. Also, although villas accounted, perhaps, for most of the land being taken for housing at that time, there were a number of terraces (of houses of varied sizes) being built as well; they can still be seen in Milford Hill, Rampart Road, Hillview Road, Kelsey Road, the lower part of Elm Grove Road, Manor Road and Fairview Road. The Commissioners were in a commanding position to exercise control in both areas (the pace and nature of development) but there is no evidence that they did so. In August 1878 they conveyed 14 acres of land to Edward Kelsey and only three months later conveyed another 29 acres to John Turner.[26] There were no restrictive conditions imposed. On Kelsey's land were built the houses in Manor Road and Fairview Road, as well as those on the east side of London Road between Kelsey Road and Weeping Cross (except the site of Kelsey House, which was retained for a Rectory). Turner's land was bounded by Wain-a-long Road, the railway and London Road.

Two new and imposing school buildings appeared at this time. The first was in Bourne Avenue, on a part of Turner's land, for the school now called Chafyn Grove School. It had been founded in 1879 by Mr W. C. Bird as the Salisbury School for Boys, in a building that comprises the southern part of the one that can be seen today. It derives its present name from Miss Julia Chafyn Grove of Zeals House near Mere. She had already endowed a ward at the Infirmary and donated funds to purchase the organ still in use at the Cathedral, and, when she died in 1897, bequeathed £500 to assist education in the City of Salisbury. The money was used to purchase the Salisbury School then privately owned and being run, very successfully, by Rev. J. C. Alcock. The change of name occurred in 1916 when it became a preparatory school. But after only two years the school buildings were requisitioned for RAF Southern Area HQ; the school was closed and the boys transferred to a school in Sussex. Chafyn Grove started afresh in 1919. After these first forty years of fluctuating fortunes and pupil numbers, the school would now settle down and undergo a period of growth and development that has been sustained to the

26  The WSRO refs are Bishoprick 183 and 200. Turner's full names were John Edmund Unett Phillipson Turner Turner.

*Chafyn Grove School (right), with detail of floor tile in entrance porch (below, left). The School was originally founded in 1879 by Mr W. C. Bird as the Salisbury School*

present day. By 1950 pupil numbers first reached 100 and currently stand at nearly 300. The school became co-educational in 1980.[27]

The other was a new home for The Godolphin School, opened in 1891 at the top of Milford Hill on a site conveyed to it by the Ecclesiastical Commissioners. An account of the school's previously nomadic existence is given in Chapter 7. There was actually a third, now largely forgotten, independent school for boys founded on Milford Hill at this time – the Cleveland House School that opened in 1880 in a large house in Kelsey Road on the eastern side of its junction with Fairview Road, a site now occupied by blocks of flats. It was soon re-

27   This account is based on information kindly supplied by the school.

*An early photograph of the Modern School, founded in 1880 as Cleveland House School at the corner of Kelsey Road and Fairview Road.*

named The Modern School but by the time of its closure in 1960 had become Cleveland School.

Meanwhile, in the old Milford, the so-called manor house (actually a farm) was acquired by George Gerrish and, in 1900, demolished and replaced by a private residence by his son, Richard Gerrish, in the semblance of a Tudor Castle. Because of Gerrish's association with the silk and cloth trade, the locals knew it as 'Calico Castle'. During the Second World War it was used by Southern Command and, from 1950, as the headquarters of the engineering firm Reed and Mallik. In 1984 it became a nursing home and in 1986 the southern part of the grounds was sold for housing and a small estate of 'executive' houses was built comprising Milford Manor Gardens. At the end of the 19th century a forge had been established on the opposite corner of Milford Mill Road by Nathaniel Barber, who was a carpenter, wheelwright and undertaker with other premises in Salisbury. In 1904 the business was transferred

*Nathaniel Barber (on right) working at the forge he established late in the 19th century on the corner of Milford Mill Road (opposite Milford Manor).*

further down the road to 9 Milford Mill Road. It was operated as a foundry by three generations of Barbers until 1990, when it closed and the site was redeveloped as a small close of detached houses.

Perhaps it should also be mentioned here that some houses were already in existence well before 1800 just outside the chequers on the east side of the town. William Naish's fine map of Salisbury (1716 and 1751 editions) shows some buildings along the bottom of the hill on the east side of Rampart Road (including the 'Winchester Gate' inn), the lower end of Milford Hill and between St Ann's Street and St Martin's church. However, all of these constituted minor extensions to the street pattern of Salisbury or St Martin rather than the first stages of the creation of a new suburb. It is a matter of degree, perhaps, but two other dwellings of about 1800 that *were* more distinctly separated from the city were the pair of cottages on the north side of Milford Hill just above the entrance to the driveway of Milford Hill House (which, therefore, they pre-date). The cottages appear in a drawing by John Constable of 1820 called *A Road Leading into Salisbury*. That the road in question is Milford Hill is apparent from a

'A Road Leading into Salisbury' by John Constable (1820).

watercolour (probably of the 1840s) *Salisbury from Milford Hill* by W. J. Gray: although the scenes differ considerably in their content, both pictures show a distinct pair of brewery buildings with high conical tops that stood at the junction of Milford Street and Culver Street.[28]

It was as a result of the building that took place from 1865 onwards that the presence here of early humans (referred to in Chapter 2) was discovered, although the full chain of relevant events is quite long. Salisbury's medieval system of water channels had finally been

28 I am grateful to Ann Harries who observed the similarity from illustrations on pp. 60 and 61 of *The Grays of Salisbury* by Donald C. Whitton.

*'Salisbury from Milford Hill' by W. J. Gray (1840s?).*

abandoned ten years before and began to be filled in. The channels had been established in the 13th century as an integral part of the city's layout, but had proved increasingly difficult to maintain. After a cholera outbreak in 1849, in which 192 people died (making it the worst-afflicted town in Britain as a percentage of population), it was finally recognised that polluted water was the likely cause of the disease and that a modern system of sewerage should be provided.[29] It had been a struggle to bring about this result. There were a few in the city like Dr Andrew Middleton who had long seen the need for better sanitary arrangements, but they had to fight against an official attitude and vested interests that were more concerned about the effect on the pockets of local ratepayers. Middleton organised a petition in 1850 seeking a Board-of-Health inspection of the town (which, eventually, took place) and one of those who signed it was Dr Richard Fowler.

One result of draining the watercourses was that it allowed the recovery of small items like keys, buckles and badges that had been accidentally dropped into the streams over the course of several centuries.

29 A sign of the ignorance that prevailed about the disease was the occasional advertisement at this time in the *Salisbury and Winchester Journal* under the heading 'Cholera and Bowel Complaints in General' for Dicey & Co.'s True Daffy's Elixir; dicey and daffy are indeed how we might regard such measures today.

Different collections of these objects came to be formed, the largest by Mr Edward Brodie of the family who once owned the *Salisbury and Winchester Journal*. A group of far-sighted people (of whom Dr Fowler was the most prominent) acquired the 'Brodie' collection, and this together with other finds became the basis of a future museum, which was duly established in 1861, first on a temporary basis at 1 Castle Street,[30] and more permanently in 1864 in St Ann's Street (where it contained a 'Fowler' Room). The collection was known as 'the drainage collection' and still forms an important part of the collections at the current home of the Salisbury & South Wilts Museum at the 'King's House' in the Close. At the same time, a second museum was being established by William Blackmore to house items from the Stone Age that he had collected in North America and elsewhere. When it was completed in 1867, its management was handed over to the Salisbury & South Wilts Museum but with Blackmore continuing its funding. He had appointed his brother Dr Humphrey Blackmore (a physician in the city) and his brother-in-law Mr E. T. Stevens as honorary curators of his museum and, upon the merger, they became two of nine honorary curators of the Salisbury, South Wilts and Blackmore Museum.

By the 1860s archaeology had already made great advances, especially in Wiltshire where it had been pioneered by antiquaries such as John Aubrey, William Cunnington and Sir Richard Colt Hoare. It is fortunate that just as the development on Milford Hill got under way there were people in Salisbury with enough knowledge and enthusiasm to undertake what would now be called 'rescue archaeology' in this important location. The building work that was taking place there involved a large number of excavations of the ground – for the footings and basements of the buildings and for the digging of gravel for use in building construction. Dr Blackmore understood the implications of this and maintained, in current terminology, a 'watching brief'. He and Stevens and those that succeeded them in this work were rewarded by the discovery of 318 axe heads. All but nine were within the area of Higher Terrace Gravel (see Map 1) and all were from the early Stone Age ('Lower Palaeolithic'), perhaps 200-250,000 years ago. Milford Hill ranks with sites in East Anglia for producing some of the earliest discoveries of palaeoliths in the mid-19th century. This was at a time when, contrary to the pre-Darwinian religious orthodoxy, it was suddenly becoming realised that they were evidence for the great antiquity of the human species. What do the finds show? Perhaps only that small bands of people

30 This property had been acquired by the promoters of the Market Hall venture; the two southern bays were demolished but the remainder was available for other uses.

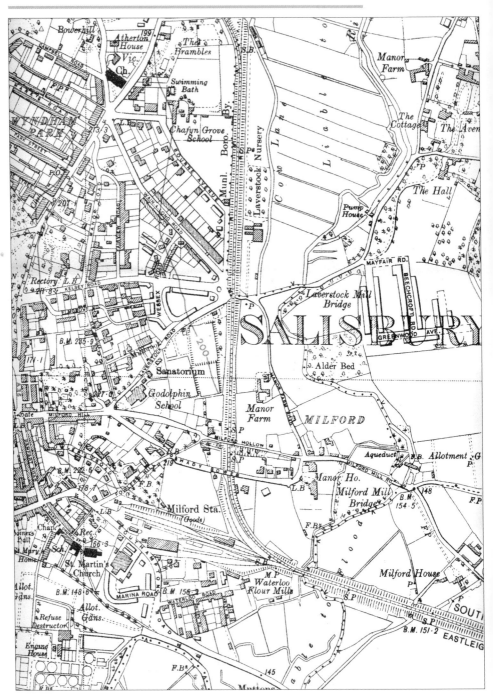

came here on different occasions over a very long period of time –
certainly not that there was a settlement here, nor even some kind of
gathering place, since they were nomadic.

# Milford

*[Opposite] Map 4: Extract from Ordnance Survey map 66SE published 1946 showing Milford as it was before the next surge of building and redevelopment.*

At the end of the First World War there was still a large tract of land on the east side of the hill between Laverstock Road and Wain-a-long Road that remained undeveloped. It was acquired by the City Council to meet a growing need for housing in the city, and from 1922 it was laid out as an estate of semi-detached houses each with a good size garden. Only the council houses in Macklin Road, begun in August 1921, are earlier than these. Little building land remained at that stage and the only other development between the wars amounted to filling some gaps. Since World War II, and especially after about 1960, Milford's Victorian suburb has undergone the same sort of changes as many across England: the villas were seen to be too large for modern living and were either subdivided into flats or apartments or were demolished. Where the building itself has survived – and many have done so – its grounds have in many cases been subdivided and one or more new dwellings erected. All the terraces have survived, which shows how well they were built and how they have continued to serve present-day housing needs.

The most significant development since the war has been the building in 1952 of St Martin's Church of England Primary School with its own grounds and playing field on a site south of Shady Bower and east of Fowler's Hill. Its initial intake was the boys from the 'old' St Martin's School (adjoining St Martin's churchyard) and the girls from St Martin's Girls School, which was then in premises in Milford Street (now a second-hand furniture store). The spaciousness and practical modern design of the new school must have been greatly appreciated by staff and pupils alike. More recently the premises have been extended to cater for the St Martin's Infants School that was still occupying the 'old' school. This had been founded in 1811 as Salisbury's first National School. The building, later extensively redeveloped, had once been a malthouse and had housed French prisoners during the Peninsular War.

# 5
# Milford Hollow and the Clarendon Way

**A** KEY FEATURE of Milford is the east–west route that first passed through it a thousand or more years ago; and still passes through it today in its modern guise as a length of the Clarendon Way long-distance footpath between Winchester and Salisbury. In Chapter 1 the route was described as passing over the ford (or bridge) across the River Bourne before proceeding to Fisherton Bridge to the west. Expressed in terms of present-day streets, the route, from east to west, was equivalent to Milford Mill Road, Milford Hollow, Milford Hill, Milford Street and New Canal. (We shall return in a moment to the last short stretch before Fisherton Bridge.) Long before the creation of New Sarum this is the route that would have been used by travellers seeking to reach Wilton (or beyond) from the direction of Winchester. The small Saxon town of *Searoburh* or *Searobryg* that pre-dated the Norman Salisbury (i.e. at Old Sarum) is unlikely to have drawn travellers away from their route, but once it had been transformed after the Conquest into the chief place in Wiltshire it would certainly have affected the pattern of travel in the area. Travellers from the Winchester direction were likely to have reached Old Sarum by a route that broadly followed the former Roman route, crossing the river at Ford. Those crossing at Milford would then turn north and reach Old Sarum via Bishopsdown.

All this would change again less than 150 years on with the planting of the new city and the building of the new cathedral, and the old route would recover its former importance. Indeed, its existence would influence the layout of the city. Salisbury's massive and all-important Market Place would be sited at the junction of two existing routes. One was the east–west road from Milford; the other was the north–south road between Old Sarum and *Aeliff's Wade* (Ayleswade). While the site was still open countryside, the road from Milford probably took a straight line to Fisherton Bridge. The double kink between the end of New Canal and the bridge may have come about only when the Market Place was laid out. In the city's early days Milford Street and New Canal had the name Winchester Street. Properties adjoining the street were referred to as 'Winchester Street upon the ditch' or 'Winchester Street by the bars' according to whether they lay west or east of the point at which the Town Ditch made its turn to the south. By the 16th century the route to Winchester went via St Thomas's Bridge and the name Winchester became and remains attached to the parallel street to the north, while the former Winchester Street became Milford Street and New Canal.

The significance of all this to the road across Milford Hill is that, certainly up to the 16th century, it was a well-used route of regional importance. Apart from lying on the route from Winchester to Wilton (and later New Sarum), it was also part of the route between the new city and the royal palace of Clarendon, which lay less than two miles east of Milford Bridge. We know that Henry III paid several visits to the cathedral while it was under construction, in particular for its consecration in 1258. On each occasion he would have ridden from Clarendon, with his retinue, through Milford Hollow and down Milford Hill into the city. Or if he wished to avoid travelling through the Market Place and High Street he could have forked left in Milford Hollow and taken the route down through the present line of Fowler's Hill to reach St Ann's Street and St Ann's Gate. Elias of Dereham would frequently have passed this way because he was working for the king on building work at Clarendon and Winchester, at the same time as overseeing construction work at Salisbury Cathedral. It is also reasonable to assume that the bulk of the provisions for the palace would have come from Salisbury including, perhaps, much of the wine that filled the prodigious wine cellar at Clarendon. The laden carts would all have trundled up Milford Hill and down the other side through the Hollow to reach Milford Bridge. Coming the other way would have been waggons carrying timber from the forest for use in the cathedral and the growing city.

And so it was that Milford Hollow and Milford Hill became 'holloways', or sunken roads formed as a result of long usage and occasional heavy rain to loosen and wash away the top surface. The same

*Statue erected in Salisbury cathedral in 1946 of Elias of Dereham: he would frequently have travelled along Milford Hollow while working both at the cathedral and at Clarendon Palace and Winchester.*

phenomenon can be seen in Fowler's Hill, which also comprises the line of a route that has been used for at least 800 years.[31] Its depth must have been more apparent after a footbridge was built across the deepest section linking Dr Fowler's house with the garden on the other side of the road. It is shown on the Ordnance Survey map of 1900 and was probably built at the end of the 19th century. Brian Barber in the 1930s often rode a horse and cart down Fowler's Road, making deliveries to Milford station from his father's foundry (see Chapter 4). He recalls that the bridge was of a

*Painting by Edwin Young (late 19th century) of Milford Hollow from its eastern end (ref. EY325).*

31  On the other side of the River Bourne, the same effect can be seen in Queen Manor Road, as it rises away from the river towards Potters Way; and also in the Clarendon Way as it rises towards Clarendon Palace, though here it is now difficult to detect as in 2005 the holloway was filled in.

*Painting by Edwin Young (late 19th century) of Milford Hollow looking east (ref. EY400.10): the wall (on left) and the footbridge over the railway are the same today but the gabled 'Milford Grove' (centre) has been replaced by Shady Bower Close.*

timber 'criss-cross' pattern, was always painted grey and was high enough to allow a loaded hay wagon to pass underneath. It was still there after the war but it is not shown in the Ordnance Survey map of 1954, so it may have been removed when St Martin's Junior School was built in 1952.

Early in the 1970s, the deepest hollowed sections of Milford Hollow were filled in, partly by the city council and partly by The Godolphin School, who owned the section west of the railway line. They were being used for fly tipping and had become a nuisance. An indication of the original depth may be seen on each side of the railway line within the railway security fences. Edwin Young made a number of paintings of the Hollow at the end of the 19th century, the most dramatic being a view looking westwards up the line of the Hollow from a point near its eastern end. By then, any use of the original road had been abandoned and a footpath had been formed along the top of its northern side. During World

War II the hollows contained a number of Nissen huts to accommodate army personnel.

The nature of Milford Hill as a holloway is still apparent. Its northern footway runs at a much higher level than the carriageway (until a point opposite the end of Fowler's Road) and near the top of the road several of the terraced houses are also raised well above the carriageway and pavement on the south side. Even before the carriageway here was tarmacadamed, it must have been wider and better maintained than the Hollow for it to have survived in its present form. It is ironic that the only surfacing that the Hollow has ever received was a few years ago to make it pleasanter to walk on as a footpath, centuries after its surface had been worn to destruction by the traffic it was required to take. This was undoubtedly the reason for the creation of Shady Bower, perhaps in the 16th or 17th century, to serve as a by-pass to the Hollow, which had become impassable for wheeled traffic.[32] For the same reason, adjoining buildings, as they have been replaced, have 'turned their backs' to the Hollow, gaining access to Shady Bower instead. The lower section had apparently been abandoned as a carriageway by 1857 because, when the Hollow was severed by the railway in that year, only a footbridge was built across it, in contrast to the vehicular bridge across Shady Bower. But the upper section, where the hollows were not so severe, was being used for vehicular access to the properties that remained there until well into the twentieth century. There is a photograph of 1913 showing a wagonette 'driven by a smartly dressed coachman' emerging from the top of the Hollow by the side of 'Rose Villa'.

32  Though it seems it was at first only for the benefit of Milford Manor since it is described in a deed of 1860 as 'the ancient private way leading from Milford Hill to Milford Manor'. [WSRO ref. CCBishoprick 171/10]. However, it is more likely that it was by then being regarded as public rather 'private' in view of the way the two routes were treated in 1857 (see main text).

# 6
# The Railways

**S**ALISBURY RAILWAY STATION with its six platforms comprises an important railway 'crossroads', standing both on the London–Exeter line and the Portsmouth–Cardiff line. But curiously Salisbury's first railway station was on the other side of the town and now only a few clues exist as to its former existence. It was in Southampton Road (now Tollgate Road) on the southern edge of Milford Hill and close to St Martin's church. It was called – not Salisbury or St Martin, as it might well have been – but Milford Station, and operated as a terminus. It opened in 1847 as part of the network of the London & South Western Railway (LSWR) linking Salisbury to Eastleigh (or Bishopstoke, as the station was then known) allowing a connection to London. There was no doubt mounting excitement in Salisbury as the track was laid and the station platform constructed. There had been a trial run from Bishopstoke as far as 'the clay-cutting at Alderbury' on 9th December 1846.[33] On 21st January a special train arrived from London carrying railway officials and 'all the London newspapers'. On 27th January 'Bison' Class *Rhinoceros* under the charge of the driver of the Royal train ran into Milford Station with 23 wagons. The opening ceremony was performed by Mr W. J. Chaplin, who was not only chairman of LSWR but had also been elected MP for Salisbury two days before. He proceeded to distribute 50 tons of coal among the poor, a reminder of the hard times that existed then in Salisbury, with its workhouses and a growing problem of insanitary and overcrowded living conditions that would lead

33  I am grateful to Sue Johnson for this information from a report in the *Salisbury Journal* 12 December 1846. It also states that 'the first Salisbury passenger by the line was Mr. Buckell, dentist of this City, who having been on a professional visit to Romsey, availed himself of this mode of conveyance to return to his residence.'

to the serious cholera epidemic of 1849. The carrying of passengers would have to await Board of Trade inspection.[34] This duly occurred on 23rd February and public services commenced on 1st March.

It was this 'public' opening that was to be the excuse for a celebratory dinner that evening at the 'White Hart' hotel in Salisbury. During the early years of Railway Mania it had seemed that the railway might never reach the city, as one scheme after another either stopped short of Salisbury or foundered altogether.[35] Thus the relief and enthusiasm of the leading citizens were very real and were expressed in heartfelt terms. A series of speeches emphasised the many benefits and the prosperity that would flow from this immense opportunity, prosperity that Mr Alford, the Chapter Clerk, hoped would be felt by the many and not just the few. In proposing the toast 'the Magistrates of the city', Mr R. M. Wilson said he saw no reason why the city 'should not again, with the present prospects before them, become as renowned for trade and commerce as it had been in former days – and, if they pulled all together, become, as had been happily expressed, "the Manchester of the South"'.

*Milford Goods Station in July 1939 with the spires of Salisbury cathedral and St Martin's church in the background.*

34  Thus making Mr. Buckell's little venture [note 33] all the more surprising.
35  In 1845, the Dean and Chapter were served with official notices in relation to land in Milford for three schemes in addition to the one that went ahead. The others were (i) a line from Cheltenham to Southampton and Poole (ii) a line from Oxford to Salisbury (iii) a line to link the LSWR line from Southampton to the Wilts, Somerset and Weymouth line.

These words were cheered – but then so were many others as the evening proceeded with one toast after another. They did not know when to stop. One might have expected 'The Ladies' to signal an end to the evening but there followed 'Foxhunting', and then 'Mr Blake's Harriers', '&c. &c', and, it will come as no surprise, 'the hilarity of the evening – one of the happiest ever passed in Salisbury – was kept up till a late hour.'[36]

The reference to Manchester and its warm reception are telling. That fast-growing city represented, it seems, everything to which many of Salisbury's leading citizens aspired – technological innovation and commercial success as well as local civic pride and a spirit of independence. Yet by now the scale of the human misery and deprivation that industrialisation had brought to Manchester, the squalor, the insanitary housing, the high mortality rate, were becoming more widely recognised. It is no wonder, however, that these were disregarded when Salisbury's own problems of sanitation were being neglected. One senses that Mr Alford's remarks were swept aside in the general euphoria.

In 1857, a line arrived from Andover providing a more direct link to London. This also used Milford Junction, as it then became known. The line ran along the east side of Milford Hill, chopping through its south-eastern corner in a cutting, requiring bridges over Milford Hollow and Shady Bower. However, the cutting may, in part at least, have been made along the line of an existing depression. In her recollections of her time at The Godolphin School as a pupil, Miss Mary Andrews, a future headmistress of the school, recalls that 'behind the school garden' there was 'a deep glen called "Switzerland"' and that when the line was begun 'the two bridges across this glen were necessary' and that '"Switzerland" is gone, never to return'. It is tempting to assume that she is referring to the deep 'glen' along the line of Milford Hollow but her description of the bridges going *across* the glen implies that this depression must have been at right angles to Milford Hollow.

Because the station was configured towards the south-west, trains would have had to run past it and then reverse in, with complications of engines having to be detached and moved around. But after the Yeovil line opened in 1859 all passenger traffic was transferred to the new station on the other side of town at Fisherton, via Tunnel Junction and the new tunnel that was cut through the southern end of Bishopsdown.[37] This left Milford as a goods station only, which it continued to be until it was closed in 1967. It is as 'Milford Goods Station' that it is most often referred to.

36  *Salisbury & Winchester Journal*, 6 March 1847, p.2.
37  This junction and tunnel, as well a line from the Andover direction, had been envisaged earlier since all appear on a map of 1845 [WSRO ref CC 31].

Since its closure, the site has been re-developed for a mixture of light industrial and leisure uses.

Milford was a busy station and an engine was kept shunting 24 hours a day. Many cattle trucks came here and there were cattle pens at the station. Sheep and cows would be driven through the streets to the Market Place, not without its hazards to passers by, right up until the 1950s – via Tollgate Road and Rampart Rd and then either Milford Street or Winchester Street. The station also had large coal bunkers and the dust would go up all over the road when it was unloaded from the trucks – hence the unusual dual name of the adjoining public house, 'The Railway Inn' *and* 'The Dust Hole'. It was built to serve the railwaymen accommodated in newly-built terraced houses (which have survived) in Waterloo Rd to the south and the two shorter streets leading off it. There was also a pair of railway cottages built in Shady Bower on the west side of the cutting ('Nos. 1 and 2 Railway Cottages, Shady Bower'), which were demolished and replaced with a new pair of houses in about 1970.

*The intensive use of Milford Station as a coal storage depot gave rise to the double name of the 'Railway Inn' and the 'Dust Hole' at the corner of Tollgate Road and Blakey Road.*

On 3rd April 1858, the *Salisbury & Winchester Journal* reported the total destruction by fire 'last Saturday night' of the passenger station. Despite difficulties in fighting the fire due to inadequate water supply, the goods station 'on the opposite side of the road' was saved (which seems to imply that, before the passenger function was transferred to Fisherton in 1859, the passenger and goods stations were operated separately and were divided by some sort of internal roadway). A temporary station for passengers was quickly erected and trains continued to run on time. We are told that 'the scene could only be compared to a huge pyrotechnic display' and that the heat was so intense that 'gold and silver left in the clerk's desk were found among the ruins on Sunday completely fused'.[38]

The station had first opened just before Milford Hill started to be built up as a suburb of Salisbury, which, as we have seen, began in a serious way in 1865. However, the houses nearest to the station would have had a lot of noise, fumes and dust to endure, and the very first to be built on the slopes of the hill overlooking the site, perhaps twenty or thirty years before the station opened, was Dr Fowler's. He could hardly have chosen a worse spot to site his house when he had so much land to play with. One hopes that his keen desire for progress helped to alleviate these impositions at the end of his life. Not all landowners yielded readily to the loss of land. The Duke of Hamilton (Lord Farmer of Milford) issued a lawsuit against LSWR and had a map drawn showing proposed building plots for villas on the southern slopes of Milford Hill below Fowler's Hill and Shady Bower.[39] The intention, presumably, was to demonstrate the potential value of the land and to increase the amount of compensation accordingly, a procedure that continues to the present day where land is acquired for public purposes.

The presence of the goods station led to the building of the Waterloo Flour Mills at the end of Waterloo Road. The premises were later taken over by The Tintometer Ltd. Activity in the area of the station was intensified during WWII with the arrival of two adjoining oil depots, first Esso and later Shell, on the north side of Waterloo Road. The buildings were of silvery appearance in an attempt to camouflage them. In the build up to D-Day, there was a constant flow of service lorries until late at night.[40] Both sites have now been made safe and redeveloped for housing.

38  Again, my thanks to are due to Sue Johnson for this information.

39  WSRO ref CC32.

40  Based on the recollections of Vera Smith, (née Hounsome) who lived in Waterloo Road throughout the war.

# 7
# The Godolphin
# School

THERE WERE THREE important sets of changes that affected
Milford in the 19th century: the eastward expansion of Salisbury,
the coming of the railways and, equally as important in its way, the arrival
of The Godolphin School. The school had been founded in 1726, but only
in the sense that that was the year Elizabeth Godolphin, the co-benefactor,
made her will. The other benefactor was her husband Charles who had
predeceased her. They left money for the foundation of a school 'for the
better education and maintenance of eight young Gentlewomen who were
to be brought up at Sarum or some other town in the county of Wilts'.
(This is duly spelt out in a lengthy inscription in a wall tablet,
commemorating the life of both donors, in the cloisters of Westminster
Abbey.)[41] The charity was to be administered by William Godolphin, a
nephew of Elizabeth. In 1721 the Dean & Chapter of Salisbury Cathedral
had declined any involvement, as vividly related in a play written for the
200th anniversary of the will in which the idea of educating young women
was ridiculed by the Dean and members of the Chapter as 'mere foolery
and dreaming'.

The school was not actually set up until 1784 – in Rosemary Lane
in the Close. It remained in the Close moving first to 'Arundells' and, in
1836, to the 'King's House'. In 1848, perhaps in fear of a cholera outbreak
(which, as we have seen, did indeed occur in 1849), it was transferred to
Milford – not to the building we see today, which is actually its fourth
home there, but to 'Milford Villa' (soon to be called 'Milford Grove') in

---

41   The tablet refers to '*orphan* gentlewomen'. The terms of the will itself are
     ambiguous on this point but by 1783 the term orphan was being used in the
     terms of the charity.

*Shady Bower Close, the site of the 'Punch Bowl' inn, which later, rebuilt as 'Milford Villa', became the first home in Milford of The Godolphin School.*

Shady Bower. It had been built a few years before on the site of the 'Punch Bowl' inn, which we have already encountered. This Milford Grove must not be confused with a present-day house of the same name only two doors away, but not built until 1925. The move was apparently beneficial from a health point of view: Miss Margaret Bazeley, who was headmistress at the time of the move, wrote in 1854:

> During the seven years of my residence on [Milford] Hill, neither myself nor pupils have required medical assistance. On the contrary, no year passed without it the whole twelve years I resided in the Close.

In 1854 the school moved to the 'White House', which was described by Miss Mary Andrews (see Chapter 5) as being 'beyond Shady Bower' and, to date, remains unidentified. (There is a house currently known as 'White Lodge' in Shady Bower but, apart from the fact that it is hardly 'beyond' Shady Bower, it was not built until 1936.)[42] After using temporary accommodation in Endless Street, Godolphin, in

42 It began life as *East End* and was later called *Tai-Mo-Shan* when it became the family home of Mr C.R. Baker, proprietor, and son of the founder, of Chas. H. Baker, men's outfitters of Milford Street.

1867, moved to a new building in Elm Grove that was named 'Fawcett House', in recognition of the contribution that had been made to the school as a governor by Sarah Maria Fawcett, the elder sister of Professor Henry Fawcett, whose statue is in the Market Place.

The school was still very small. Miss Andrews reports that, when she became headmistress in 1875, there were eleven pupils. By 1886, numbers had increased to 'sixteen or eighteen boarders, which was as many as the Elm Grove house would hold.' But also from that time, the number of 'day scholars' began to increase and two years later, plans for a new school building were being discussed. The new building was designed for eighty girls and, according to another former pupil, 'the cabbage field at the top of Milford Hill with one chestnut tree was soon in the hand of builders, and the new red school rose up'.

The new building was opened in 1891 and would soon be extended. The way in which it grew 'organically' is well described by Miss C. R. Ash, headmistress from 1919:

> The building grew to meet the growth of the living organism that it had been formed to house: there was no sudden new development, no large and complete plan adopted, but as the numbers increased and funds became a little more elastic an improvement was effected here or there, rooms were adjusted to other uses and fresh space found for the old needs. Thus one thing led to another . . .

Indeed it did, and has continued to do so ever since, as the site has grown into a large school campus, now containing a series of buildings representative of most decades. Some of them replace buildings that the school had previously used on other sites within Milford, with the result that most activities have now been consolidated within its principal site (bounded by Milford Hollow, Laverstock Road and the railway line) or very close to it. But, both before and since 1891, the school's constant need for suitable boarding houses has been an important element of the life of Milford and the way it has developed.[43] The presence of so many large Victorian houses met the need well and a great number of them were used at different times, from Dr Fowler's old house in the south to 'Cedar House' that once stood at the north end of Manor Road. The provision of purpose-built boarding accommodation began with 'Douglas House', in Laverstock Road, in 1961.

The staff and pupils have long made up a significant part of Milford's population, something that would have been more evident

43  By contrast, Chafyn Grove School (and its predecessor, the Salisbury School) was always able to meet all its needs within its ample grounds.

when the boarding houses were more widely spread. From about 1960 onwards, when large Victorian houses were no longer wanted for family use, the disposal by the school of one of its houses would often be the opportunity for its demolition and replacement by a denser scheme of housing. One exception is 'Inwood House' (formerly 'Jerred House', and, as we shall see in the next chapter, originally called 'Holmleigh'). After the school required it no longer this was acquired for use as a retirement home. Two older buildings that have been retained are 'School House' in The Avenue and 'Rose Villa', the wedge-shaped house between the Hollow and Shady Bower. The latter was originally acquired as the school's Kindergarten and now houses its Music Department, accounting for the sound of flute, piano or violin that can often be heard wafting though its windows.

*The Godolphin School today, with name board incorporating the arms and Cornish motto of the Godolphin family.*

The board at the entrance to the school displays the arms of Godolphin, the family of Cornish origin of which both Charles and Elizabeth were distantly related members. This explains the curious motto '*Franc ha leal eto ge*', which looks as if it might be Norman French but is actually Cornish. Since there have been no native speakers of the language for more than 200 years it is not surprising that the motto exists in different forms, but the school's own research concluded that there was 'now little doubt' that this was the correct one. It means 'frankness and loyalty be thine'. Another allusion to the Godolphin name is the weather vane at the top of a gable on the main school building: it is meant to be a dolphin although you could be excused for thinking it was a whale.

The original eight pupils have increased to about 420 today. Perhaps the most distinguished Old Godolphin is the author Dorothy L.

Sayers who was a pupil in the early years of the last century. She wrote a semi-autobiographical story *Cat O'Mary* (not published until 2002) based on her experiences. Also, a published collection of her letters includes many written from the school. They throw light on her early passion for language and literature but unfortunately very little on her surroundings. She does, however, write of a visit in 1909 to Old Sarum and of one, on or about her 17th birthday (19th June) in 1910, to the Woodford valley. The visit to Old Sarum was 'to see the excavations' i.e. those undertaken in 1909–14 under Sir William Hope and others. She reports to her mother that 'they have uncovered some *lovely* perfect walls, and a postern gate . . . and have found lots of Norman and Roman pottery and iron-work . . . I am sending Aunt Mabel some relics. I hope they will arrive safely . . .'

The 1910 visit was 'to a place called Lake . . . somewhere near Stonehenge, I think'. She tells her mother that 'we had been invited to tea by some dear little people who live the simple life in a little house on the top of a hill, overlooking the most perfect scenery. The old grandfather, whose name is Mr Lovibond, is most awfully clever, and a perfect old dear. He owns Lake House – a glorious old place,[44] but he has let it and built himself this sweet little house on the hill.' It would seem that it was not just her knowledge of local geography that was incomplete but that she was unaware that this was Joseph Lovibond, the inventor of the colorimeter (or tintometer as he called it) that he and his successors developed into an internationally accepted system for grading colour. In recent times the premises of The Tintometer Ltd lay at the east end of Waterloo Road, mentioned in Chapter 6 for its railway cottages.[45] Nor, for that matter, would Lovibond have been aware that this young woman would become a world-famous author. She alluded to Salisbury in her first novel, *Whose Body?*, in which Lord Peter Wimsey visits a solicitor in Milford Street, first lunching in the Minster [Cathedral] Hotel in the same street.

Mary Andrews' association with the school, first as a pupil and later as headmistress, straddled the years that saw Milford transformed from countryside to suburb. This is how she recalled the surroundings of the school in the 1850s:

44  A view no doubt shared by its present resident, Gordon Sumner, the musician better known as Sting. The Elizabethan house seen by Sayers was gutted by fire in 1912 but was carefully restored for Lovibond by the architect, Detmar Blow.

45  The company moved to Amesbury in 2006 and the buildings were demolished in 2007.

Laverstock, Clarendon, Bishopsdown, the Southampton and London Roads, all these were quite country. Shut your eyes and try and picture no houses between the part of Milford Street where the old ditch runs (or did run) to Nelson House itself [a school house that fronted the Hollow]; no Fowler's Road, only the house from which it takes its name, then inhabited by an old Dr. Fowler; and, in the other direction, really an Elm Grove with gardens and fields behind two white mud walls on each side of a narrow muddy lane where Millbrook is, but not a single house to be seen, fields and downs stretching away on the right above the Greencroft, and on the left a real Wyndham's Park with glorious beech trees overhanging the low wall which ran all along to the little toll-gate which stood at Weeping Cross Corner – more fields, more downs, bleak, bare, breezy, the very thought of which brings back the lark's song to one's ears, and the scent of wild thyme, and the vision of the white saxifrage and tender blue hare-bell . . .

The 'old ditch' was that which used to run along what is now Rampart Road. In her recollection of an absence of houses beyond Milford Street Miss Andrews seems to have ignored the houses at the bottom of Milford Hill, but her account of countryside so close to the edge of the city is a plausible and valuable reminder of the school's early environment.

# 8
# People

I N SALISBURY AND SOUTH WILTSHIRE MUSEUM there is a
pane of glass containing an engraved inscription that reads as follows:

> Dear Clarissa – Puellarum omnium formissima
> She's the fairest where thousands are fair

These words are preceded by what appears to be a trial run: a
capital letter D followed by a series of connected loops. A label reads
*'From the summer house of Milford Manor, Salisbury. The inscription
was probably executed by Henry Fielding'.* The pane was given to the
museum in 1978 by Reed & Mallik while they were in occupation of the
manor house (see Chapter 4). The author Henry Fielding (1707-54) is
known to have strong Salisbury connections. His grandmother lived in
Salisbury and he paid her many visits as a schoolboy and young man.
He was a friend of James Harris of
Malmesbury House in the Close and came to
know Charlotte, the daughter of 'Widow'
Cradock at No.14 on the other side of North
Walk and later married her. For a time he
served as High Steward of the New Forest.
There is a tradition that Fielding used the
summer house as a workroom and wrote part
of *Tom Jones* there. He had become a barrister
in 1740 and came to Wiltshire Assizes on the
western circuit. Salisbury was one of his
resting places at which he occupied himself
writing the novel, which was published in 1748.
However, from the pattern of his life it is
unlikely that he resided at the house (as

*Engraved inscription 'probably executed by Henry Fielding' on a windowpane (now held at the Salisbury and South Wilts Museum) from the summerhouse of Milford Manor. The photograph was taken for sale particulars in 1930 while the window was still in situ.*

*Detail of the memorial in St Martin's church to Bennett Swayne of Milford Manor and his brother Thomas. The Swayne arms displayed here also appear inside the summerhouse of Milford Manor.*

opposed to merely staying there), although Wiltshire historians have asserted that he did.[46] The most likely candidate as the occupier of the manor house at that time was Bennet Swayne (1696-1748), the last of three Bennet Swaynes 'of Milford'[47] (and the summer house contains the arms of Swayne inside above the doorway) but the link with Fielding is not known nor is the identity of Clarissa. The inscription would be more consistent with the earlier period of his life when he would pay court to the girls of the city at the Assembly Rooms in New Street while on his visits to his grandmother. Perhaps he first came to know Bennet Swayne at that time and later stayed at his house whenever he was in Salisbury.

Before we try to get a feel for the people who were coming, in ever-increasing numbers, to live in Milford during Victorian times, the nature of William Beckford's interest in Milford (its Lord Farmer) needs to be explored. It is tempting to assume that it could only have been financial, one item within many in his huge portfolio,[48] and we saw at the beginning of Chapter 3 that the lease of the Bishop's manor was, in any event, first granted to his father. The first lease of Milford directly to Beckford himself was in 1782 on his attaining his majority. It is difficult to imagine how he could ever have come to take any personal interest in Milford as a place: from the time he first inherited his father's wealth in 1770, he was either abroad (generally fleeing from some sexual scandal or another) or living a reclusive existence, first in his father's house, Fonthill Splendens, and later in Fonthill Abbey. Early in 1782 his agent had told Lady Mary Hume, the wife of the bishop, that 'by his account Mr Beckford is rather indifferent about the Renewal [of the lease]'.[49]

46  Sir Richard Colt Hoare in *History of Modern Wiltshire, the History of the Hundred of Alderbury* (1837) [in which he further asserts that this is where Fielding wrote 'part of his *Tom Jones*'] and Benson and Hatcher in *Old and New Sarum* (1843) [who say it is where he wrote 'a considerable portion of *Tom Jones*'].

47  See the family notes held at Devizes Museum, *Swaynes of Wiltshire*, written and published by Margaret K. Swayne Edwards in 1940.

48  Most of his landed assets were in Jamaica; in England he held property at Hindon, his Fonthill estate and Fonthill Bishop Farm, as lessee of the Bishop of Winchester, in addition to Milford and Woodford [see Alexander p.189].

49  Letter dated 19 January 1782 [WSRO ref CC Bishoprick 158].

And yet Tim Mowl has shown, in his book *William Beckford, Composing for Mozart*, that in the last years of his life (he died in 1844) he had plans to build a villa at Milford and, in its grounds, a mausoleum for himself, a domed building with urns at each corner and alcoves for at least eight coffins. The plans, in the Bodleian Library in Oxford, indicate no specific location. However, we can, perhaps, infer from the location of his last home, Lansdown Tower, standing high above Bath, that his villa would have been at the very top of Milford Hill, perhaps on the present site of The Godolphin School. Some evidence for this can be derived from a proposal Beckford put forward in 1832 to 'reserve for himself' four plots for the building of villas. Whist this appears to be an essentially commercial exercise – perhaps to help prop up Beckford's failing fortunes – and was one that did not succeed, it is very likely that one of the plots was later envisaged as the site of Beckford's intended villa and mausoleum. One plot was a

*Portrait of William Beckford, aged 21, by George Romney.*

triangle of land between London Road and St Mark's Avenue. Though the largest, at nearly 8 acres, it lies on the lower slopes of Bishopsdown and slopes awkwardly in two directions. The other three were all adjacent to the road junction at the top of Milford Hill. One lay between Milford Hill and Fowler's Hill; the second between Shady Bower and Milford Hollow; and the third between Milford Hollow and Laverstock Road. This last contained nearly three acres and represents the plot later acquired for The Godolphin School. It enjoys an imposing position, would then have had fine views in all directions and is likely to have been the one of greatest attraction to Beckford.

An interesting aspect of this attempt to obtain the bishop's approval to a transfer of the land to Beckford for villa development is that the map shows three acres of land between London Road and Cow Lane to the east 'considered desirable to be planted [donated] to the Lord Bishop of Salisbury for the accommodation of the Poor (if required)'. How reminiscent of the common procedure today of making a portion of land available for 'social housing' when seeking planning permission for new commercial housing development! 

Dr Richard Fowler, the first Salisbury man to build a mansion on

*Tomb of William Beckford and Lansdown Tower.*

the west side of the hill, was, perhaps, Milford's most prominent resident, and it is apt that two streets there are named after him. He was born in 1765 and died in 1863. He practised medicine in Salisbury for 60 years and was the Honorary Physician of the Infirmary for 47 years between 1794 and 1841. He was a Fellow of the Royal Society and, for 60 years, a Fellow of the Society of Antiquaries. We have seen evidence of his passion for the study and preservation of historic objects in connection with the drainage collection and the creation of a museum for Salisbury. He was keenly interested in what would later be called 'adult education' and founded and built the Working Men's Institute in St Ann's Street.

He was a friend of William Nightingale of Embley Park near Romsey. His daughter Florence, having received in 1837 what she believed to be a call from God to pursue a mission, was starting to think that that mission lay in nursing, and had broached with Fowler the possibility of her training as a nurse at Salisbury Infirmary (although he himself had retired from his position there) and of staying with his family at his house at Milford. One evening in December 1845 she put the proposal to her own family while they were at home in the company of Fowler and his wife. Nursing was then regarded as menial work suitable only for the 'working classes' and Florence's mother had the notion that hospitals were a hotbed of immorality between nurses and surgeons. Florence's proposal was not well received. Her sister Parthenope had hysterics and her mother wept at the thought of Florence wanting to 'disgrace herself' and flew into a rage. So she never did come to Salisbury at that time, though, later in life, she would advise on extensions at the Infirmary at the request of her friend Sidney Herbert, who was Chairman of the Board of Governors and who had been Secretary of State at War during the Crimean War.

Milford Hill House (now the Youth Hostel) was built for Charles Everett and would later be acquired by William Pinckney MA, JP (1834-1917). Both were associated with Pinckneys Bank. It was not William who gave his name to Pinckneys Bank in Salisbury – it had been founded in 1810 – but he became a partner in 1857 and, upon its merger with the Wilts & Dorset Bank, was made a director of that too. Pinckneys first

*Milford Hill House (c.1840) built for Charles Everett of Pinkneys Bank and later the home of William Pinckney (now a Youth Hostel).*

had premises in Tailor's Hall, Endless Street (which has been demolished) and in 1878 moved to new premises in Queen Street, which still exist as Cross Keys House. William had been born at West Amesbury in 1834, educated at Eton and Oxford, and was 'by birth and education allied to the landed gentry, sharing their pursuits and sports', as a contemporary biography puts it; but with commercial interests in the town he was one of those for whom 'as townsmen, there were no positions of dignity to which they could not aspire, while the amenities of the cultured social life of the country side were equally at their command.' He lived at Milford with his wife Frances (the daughter of Rev. G. F. Everett) and their six children. A window in the south aisle of St Edmund's Church (now Salisbury Arts Centre) contains an inscription 'in memory of William Pinckney Esq JP who levelled the Churchyard during the years 1864-1866'.

*William Pinckney (1834-1917) – resident of Milford Hill House.*

The garden of Milford Hill House backs on to an unmade street called Bellamy Lane containing three surviving Victorian villas. At the time of the 1891 census, two of them, 'Glen Lyn' and the adjoining 'Hollyhurst' (now 'Holly House'), were the homes of, respectively, James and William Moore, both 'boot manufacturers'. In 1873 they had begun trading as Moore Bros, taking over the firm of Rowe, Moore and Moore that had been established in 1820 at 51 Silver Street, Salisbury. In 1889 they had established a fine new boot and shoe factory in Southampton Road (now Tollgate Road) and by 1896 were trading from the Market Place. Moore Bros were taken over by Russell & Bromley in 1969 but continued trading under their old name at various premises in Salisbury. In 1993 they moved to Downton where they specialise in the manufacture of orthopaedic footwear.

The third house in Bellamy Lane, 'Holmleigh' (now the Inwood House Retirement Home) was the home of a solicitor, Hamilton Fulton, in 1891 but it formerly belonged to William Price Aylward, a prominent Salisbury citizen who was a former Mayor (1868/9) and of some standing in the musical world. His wife Mamie Aylward was a friend of the family of the author E. M. Forster and he used to visit 'Holmleigh' regularly as a child (while he was still known as Morgan Forster) and as a young man. He remembered it as 'a tall sun-drenched house balanced high above Salisbury'. He used to walk down to the River Bourne and beyond, to Clarendon and Figsbury Ring. The Bourne Valley and Figsbury Ring are featured in *The Longest Journey*. Also, the circumstances of Mamie's (second) marriage to Aylward made a big impression on Forster and were reflected in two of his novels, *Where Angels Fear to Tread* and *Howards End*. She had accepted a proposal from him but her family opposed the match because he was a partner in a music shop at 13 Canal Street and was therefore 'Trade'.

On the other side of The Avenue, in what is now 'School House', lived George Pepper (Lt. Col. retired) with his wife, six children, a school governess and three general servants. He had retired to Milford after serving in the Crimea, India and China. He became a leading supporter of the Salvation Army in Salisbury, something that would place him in little less physical danger than his army career. For a body of Salisbury citizens had taken exception to Salvation Army parades, forming in 1881 the Society for the Suppression of Street Parading. The following year saw violent demonstrations and Col. Pepper was so badly injured in one of them as to need hospital treatment. But by 1899 the Army had been accepted in the city and foundation stones were laid for a larger hall in Salt Lane. The names of 'Colonel G. N. Pepper' and of 'Mrs Colonel Pepper' may still be seen on two of them. When the colonel died in 1901 between 3,000 and 4,000 people crowded into the London Road cemetery to mourn a man, who, in the words of the *Salisbury Times*, 'laboured morning noon and night in the interest of the working classes of the city.'[50]

In Elm Grove in 1891 the picture was a little different. At No.1 lived George Carter, a retired whitesmith (a form of metal smith) with his wife and one servant. At No.2 there was Thomas Davis, a mineral water manufacturer with his wife, daughter, son, one servant and a Baptist minister as lodger. At No.3 Emma Mills, described as a widow and boarding house keeper, had one servant in residence with her as well as a bank clerk and an ironmonger's assistant. Amelia Offerway at No.4

50   See article by John Chandler in *Wiltshire Life* (August 2004) and Newman and Howells pp.99-100.

may have regarded herself as somewhat superior socially to her neighbour at No.3, being described as 'living on own means' and sharing her home with a companion, one servant and two clerks in holy orders.

'The Mount', Elm Grove Road, was the home of another Mayor (in 1874), Samuel Atkins JP, who had a pharmacy in the Market Place until 1896. He was a Member of the Pharmaceutical Council for over 30 years and its President in 1903. He was a Director of the Salisbury Gas Company; served on the Committee of Salisbury Infirmary and the Herbert Convalescent Home, Bournemouth; was a trustee of the Salisbury Municipal Charities; and, more impressively, perhaps, than any of these, was an Income Tax Commissioner.

As one went further north into Kelsey Road and Manor Road, there were terraces as well as villas and so there would have been a greater social mix of people. Except that the grandest houses here, set in very large plots, fronted London Road at the end of long driveways, and so those who lived in them need not have been concerned with what happened behind them. In 1891, one such resident, was Ernest Rawlence, land agent, who lived at 'Newlands' with his wife and six children and four domestic servants. At 'Rougemont' lived Arthur Whitehead, solicitor, with his wife, two children and four domestic servants.[51]

At the other end of the social scale would have been the residents of the rows of terraces in Fairview Road, tucked away in their separate world behind the houses on the east side of Manor Road. Occupations of 'heads of household' recorded in 1891 included general labourer, charwoman, gardener, agricultural labourer and railway porter. A similar picture emerges in respect of the modest 'two-up two-down' houses on the south side of Milford Hill with their tiny gardens tucked into the rising ground behind.

The Godolphin School enjoys a high national reputation and attracts pupils from afar. Yet it is essentially a local school managed by local people. Early trustees or governors included Bishop Denison, Earl Nelson (who would serve the school for 59 years),[52] Bishop Hamilton, Field-Marshal Lord Methuen (both of whom are commemorated in the names of houses), Sarah Fawcett and the Earl of Radnor, as well as two Milford residents whom we have already met, William Pinckney and

*Sarah Maria Fawcett, a distinguished governor of The Godolphin School after whom Fawcett House, the school's home before its present one, was named.*

51  These names lived on for many years in the firms of Rawlence & Squarey, estate agents, and Whitehead, Vizard, Venn & Lush, solicitors. Whitehead would have been surprised to know that his home would one day become solicitors' offices (its use today).

52  Related to Horatio Nelson's brother, William, on whom was conferred the titles of Viscount of Merton and Earl of Trafalgar and Merton in 1805 and who acquired Trafalgar House, Standlynch in 1814.

Samuel Atkins. Many of Salisbury's deans have served on the Governing Body and if, as Miss Douglas (see below) has put it, 'we draw a veil over the encounter [in 1721] between Elizabeth Godolphin and the Dean and Chapter of Salisbury', the School has 'nothing but gratitude to record for all the help that has streamed into the School from the deans and canons of the cathedral.' In 1890, Miss Andrews was succeeded by the inspirational Miss Mary Douglas, who would be the first headmistress in the new building and would remain so until 1919. She presided over a period of considerable growth and change and was held in great respect and affection both by staff and by pupils. In 1911 she brought prestige to the school when she was elected President of the Head Mistresses Conference.

The house that may have been the first to be built in Fowler's Road, in 1883, is No.31, now Byways Guesthouse. The first owner was William Cripps, whom A. G. Street called 'the prince of grocers'. He was the proprietor of a high-class grocery shop on the corner of Milford Street and Catherine Street, which has been recorded for posterity in a contemporary photograph also showing Cripps himself and an assistant standing outside in their aprons. We must not forget Richard Gerrish of Milford Manor. By the time he built his castellated mansion he was already sole proprietor of Style and Gerrish, silk and cloth merchants, which makes it surprising that the name of 'Style' should have persisted well into the second half of the twentieth century in the name of the clothing store in Blue Boar Row in Salisbury. He lived with his wife and two daughters and in 1911 became the owner of an early model of a Salisbury-made Scout motor car, a green 15hp 'landaulette', for his private use.[53] He was a governor of Salisbury Infirmary.

*Richard Gerrish, who rebuilt Milford Manor.*

53  I am grateful to Ruth Newman for this piece of information.

# 9
# All Change at Milford?

S O WHAT CAN BE SEEN in Milford today that is either of some intrinsic interest or a reminder of the past? A good starting point is Milford Bridge, which is the only official 'ancient monument' in the area and is probably little different today from when it was built in the 14th century. However, in recent years its very structure has been at risk. As recently as the 1960s the passage of a motor vehicle across the bridge was an infrequent occurrence – perhaps a few each hour. Today it is subjected to a growing flood of vehicles, running into thousands each day; some is genuine local traffic but most are using the 'rat run' to and from Southampton Road along Petersfinger Road. This route becomes increasingly attractive as traffic congestion on the roads closer to the city centre continues to grow. Some years ago, the stone pillar at the east end of the northern parapet was demolished in an accident and no repair was effected until the present traffic lights were installed for fear that the same thing would happen again if traffic movement remained uncontrolled. This accounts for the bright new stone of the present pillar and the chunk of old stone still lying by its side.

The two 18th-century 'mill' buildings on the north side of the bridge are still a picturesque feature of this part of Milford and both are 'listed'. Moving westwards down Milford Mill Road, there is now a new housing estate on the left and then another close of houses on the right on the site of R. D. Barber's foundry. The brick wall just beyond this, now acting as a high front garden wall, is what remains of a row of cottages that have otherwise been demolished. The shape of the bricked-up doors and windows can still be made out. It faces the much longer 'listed' manor house wall, originally built about 300 years ago. The section that has been rebuilt with the same mix of materials, predominantly blocks of Greensand with squares of knapped flint, should last at least as long

*The former summer-house of Milford Manor.*

again. In the older section of wall, natural weathering has caused the face of the Greensand blocks to recess by several inches in places and is likely to require attention within a few decades.

Milford Manor itself is neither listed nor of great artistic merit but its castellated turret and craggy outline are striking features of this prominent site. It was designed by Salisbury architect Fred Bath who could turn his hand to any style that was required and seemed particularly fond of historical references (he was responsible for the front of what is now the Odeon cinema in New Canal). The 'Fielding' summerhouse can be glimpsed in one of the gardens of Milford Manor Gardens. At the foot of Milford Hollow stands Little Manor, the oldest house in Milford, now another retirement home. It is an example of English Baroque from the late 17th century in the domestic style that we associate with Christopher Wren, in red brick with stone corners (that have been painted) and long sash windows on each of its two principal floors. The building has been vastly extended but with little detriment to the appearance of the original house. The only jarring note is the sight of two feeble dormer windows that have been inserted in the roof at some stage. On the opposite corner is 'Corner Cottage', a simple but pleasing 18th-century cottage where Nathaniel Barber established his forge.

So much for old Milford. Two survivors from the 18th century in Milford Hollow are the old original part of 'Brome House', which can partly be seen behind a high fence that now separates it from the Hollow, and, higher up, 'The Wilderness', which is older than the much taller 'Rose Villa' built, in the following century, hard up against its rear wall. In the parallel Shady Bower, nothing from that period has survived, unless 'The Wilderness' is included, since it has pedestrian access to both roads where they run close together at their western extremities. An image of 'Milford Grove' (formerly 'Milford Villa') distantly appears in one of Edwin Young's paintings of Milford Hollow. Today, from the same spot, we see the rectangular shapes of the Shady Bower Close blocks of flats rather than the gables of the old building.

Of the pioneering mansions on the western slope of the hill (Dr Fowler's and William Pinckney's) only the latter still exists, as the

*Painting by Edwin Young (late 19th century) of Shady Bower looking east (ref. EY305): the farm buildings on the bend of the road were removed when Milford Manor was rebuilt and the large copper beech that now dominates this view may have been planted soon afterwards.*

present-day Youth Hostel. Set in spacious grounds, it is still possible to imagine it as the home of a prosperous Victorian family, notwithstanding the intensive use that it enjoys today – up to 20,000 visitors in a year. It is a two-storey house with a typically 'Regency' ironwork veranda on two sides, emphasising the length of its front façade. The main feature of the grounds is the huge cedar tree that is probably at least as old as the house. Although Fowler's house has gone, his coach house may still be seen in Fowler's Hill (the 'Old Coach House'), having undergone an attractive dormered transformation when the rest of the site was developed for housing.

And so we come to the post-1865 Victorian suburb – and it is surprising just how many of the original buildings can still be seen. A few of the 'villas' are still family homes, but for the most part they are now either sub-divided or have some institutional use. At the south end, there is 'Grove House' in Shady Bower, 'Highmount' and 'Eastmount' at the top of Fowler's Hill and several more in the lower part of Fowler's Hill and in Fowler's Road, ranging in style from that of a Gothic Horror film to elegant Classicism. Perhaps the most pleasing is No. 31 (Byways Guesthouse) built for William Cripps in 1883 in good quality grey/yellow brick, probably from the Fisherton brickyards in Wilton Road. It boasts an elegant loggia on its north side and its front façade is liberally bestowed with the 'Aesthetic' sunflower motif that was so fashionable at that time. Beyond this point the villas give way to smaller houses that link up with the terraces of Milford Hill. But by taking the pedestrian route through the modern development on your right you can descend some steep stone steps to a point near the top of Milford Hill where once stood 'Methuen House' (formerly 'South Bank'), one of The Godolphin School's boarding houses. Its former presence is given away by the stone steps and the Victorian tiles at their base, all retained *in situ* (along with part of the front garden wall) when the building was demolished. These features lay on the route of a passage that led to 'Hamilton House' beyond (this was 'Oakhurst' before it was acquired by the school). The names of both houses live on in those of the boarding houses on the main campus.

We have already noted the cluster of villas at the southern end of Elm Grove Road and Bellamy Lane – 'Glen Lyn', 'Holly House', 'School House' and 'Inwood House'. Another is the misleadingly named 'Milford Cottage' at the top of Milford Hill, which must have been a substantial house even before it was extended. It is unusual for being in an Italianate style and for having a skin, on its three extended sides, of mathematical tiles (of which more later). The majority of the Elm Grove Estate houses still exist, the most imposing being 'The Mount'.

Manor Road's surviving villas include 'Manor House' and 'Hillcote' on the east side and Nos. 35, 43 ('Tower House'), 45 and 47 on the west. Those on the east side are both in brick but involving very different styles and building techniques. 'Manor House' is in the Norman Shaw 'Old English' style but substituting brick for the more usual timber frame construction in the upper levels; the effect of jettying of the first and second floors is achieved by the gradual projection of the brick courses at the corners of the projecting bays (a motif also deployed at 'Eastmount', Fowler's Hill). The original brick wall along the street frontage is also worthy of study. 'Hillcote' – for many years the home of St Probus School – is a much quirkier building, designed (a few years

*'Old Coach House', Milford Hill: all that remains of Dr Richard Fowler's residence.*

before Milford Manor) by Fred Bath, with bits of everything – gables, window aprons, Byzantine-like apses and even a Venetian window – and a great deal of intricately carved brickwork. For some reason, it is the only one of the villas on Milford Hill that has been listed (in 1999).

Three of the four large villas that once fronted London Road are still there, best seen from Estcourt Road, the former London Road, on the far side of the inner relief road.[54] Indeed, from here it is possible to appreciate the size of the plots in which the houses had been built, sweeping down to the road at the foot of the slope. The lower sections of the grounds were acquired for the relief road (in about 1970) and new means of access formed from Manor Road. Thus, two of the former villas, Rougemont and The Old House, are approached today from Rougemont Close off Manor Road. 'Rougemont', was the home of the staff of the Royal Commission on Historical Monuments when they were engaged on their mammoth study of Salisbury during the 1970s. It is now solicitors' offices. 'The Old House', in the exuberant Old English style, associated with the architect Norman Shaw, dripping with false beams and gables, has been converted into flats. It was formerly called 'Newlands' as can be seen by a carved stone block set into the brick wall adjoining the footpath alongside the relief road. The largest house of all, 'Kelsey House', in a style more Lutyens than Shaw, has access from Kelsey Road and is still in single occupation. The villas go on into Wain-a-long Road and Bourne Avenue, the most elegant and redolent of its era being No. 7 Wain-a-long Road, still set in spacious grounds. Those of the large No. 44 Manor Road, on the junction with Wain-a-long Road, underwent intensive development in 2006, including a curious extension into the site of the terrace of houses in Fairview Road.

'Dunraven House' in Bourne Avenue has some elaborate carved brickwork and Nos. 16, 20 and 22 are other late Victorian villas that have found new uses. A unique feature (for Milford) is the large Bath stone porch at No. 22 with Corinthian columns that are finely carved if somewhat lacking in Classical proportions. On the bend of Bourne Avenue stands Chafyn Grove School, an imposing brick pile of 1879 that seems to be taking itself more seriously than the Godolphin building built a few years later. Whereas the latter was built as a low and 'homely' Elizabethan country mansion, with large gables and mullioned windows, Chafyn Grove is cliff-like and severe, though relieved by a row of small gables below the roof line, a plain Jacobean-style porch climbing up through all its storeys and a great deal of intricate brickwork including

54  Providing an excuse, if one were needed, to visit the 'Wyndham Arms', where John Gilbert first brewed his beer in 1986, and in 1991 formed the famous Hop Back Brewery.

two pedimented aedicules (decorative features within the surface of the wall). The school stands in generous grounds, which now contain several modern buildings as well as a wide range of sporting and recreational facilities. These are best observed when travelling on the adjoining railway line.

Fairview Road is one of several parts of the 19th century development that may be overshadowed by the greater magnificence of the villas but provided many more homes than its illustrious neighbours. The same is true of the local authority housing on the eastern slopes of the hill in Wain-a-long Road, Kelsey Road and Wessex Road. The whole estate (so far as not sold under Right to Buy provisions) underwent a major refurbishment programme in 1996-97 and comprises a valuable part of the city's social housing stock. The houses are of traditional design and sound construction and will not need to be demolished and replaced like many built after WWII when speed and low cost were of paramount importance.

The number of buildings on the Godolphin School campus continues to grow. The first major project was a large new building opened as a science block in 1936. It was re-opened as an art block (by Diana, Princess of Wales) in 1991. A library was built next to the main building in 1966 and the Hamilton and Methuen boarding houses in 1974. In 1996, the round Performing Arts Centre, containing the Blackledge Theatre, was opened by Sir Timothy West. The latest major addition is another boarding house close to 'Brome House', which has itself been absorbed within the site. Each new building has been designed in its own contemporary style. The front of the site is ringed with mature trees including three chestnuts. They are what remains of a 'forest of oaks, sycamores, chestnuts, and laurels that were planted in 1892'.[55]

As well as possessing a good variety of building styles and motifs, Milford contains a good mix of building materials. Natural stone is largely confined to Milford Bridge, the old manor house wall and Milford Manor. The wall, as we have noted, is largely built of Greensand and flint but it also contains some Tisbury stone and a few bricks here and there. For the Manor House, Fred Bath adopted an unusual 'crazy-paving' style for the walls in what has been called 'Mendip granite' (probably carboniferous limestone) with Tisbury stone dressings. Its construction has stood the test of time, unlike the cheap plaster-fronted walls that were built along the Shady Bower frontage when the site was altered in the 1980s and which are already falling apart. Stone can also be found here and there elsewhere in Milford, for example in the dressings of the 1891 Godolphin building. Two cob walls survive, one along the western boundary of the Youth Hostel site and another in Shady Bower enclosing 'White Lodge'. But the predominant material, especially for the Victorian buildings, is brick. Most is red, much of it, perhaps, from Fareham, a source then of high-quality supplies, but several villas were built of the grey/yellow shade (technically known as 'white') that was produced locally in yards along Wilton Road where deposits of brick clay had been found.

One such villa was 'Holmleigh', more yellow than grey, which may be one reason that E. M. Forster recalled it as being 'sunlit'. Another form of brick, of which there are fifty or so examples in Salisbury, is the mathematical tile, used as a form of cladding but with all the appearance of brick through the cunning way it is designed and laid. Such tiles may be seen on three sides of 'Milford Cottage' and on a projection on the side of No. 45 Manor Road. Another material that was popular in Victorian times for decorative elements was terracotta. A great deal of it was used at 'The Mount', Elm Grove Road and at Nos. 14–18 Manor Road. It was also used for chimney pots and there is a fine collection, many shaped like crowns, on the terraced houses in Milford Hill, best viewed from the raised pavement on the other side of the road.

Two of Salisbury's six surviving Victorian pillar boxes are to be found in Milford including its oldest, namely, the one at the junction of Manor Road and Kelsey Road. However, from its appearance you would not even know that it is Victorian because it is an example of the Anonymous box, which, through an oversight of the manufacturers (Andrew Handyside & Co. of Derby) was not given the usual 'VR' marking. It would have been made in the period 1879 to 1883. The other

55  *Per* Gertrude Edwards (see note 25)

is at No. 96 Milford Hill[56] and dates from the period 1887 to 1904, by which time the manufacturers, Handysides, had mended their ways.

Milford has retained many of its trees. They not only add to the character of the place but provide a valuable backdrop to the view from the centre of Salisbury looking east along Milford Street. For all the change that Milford has seen over the last 150 years it is an area of Salisbury that has, on the whole, and despite some grievous mistakes, maintained a civilised balance between modern amenities and historical interest. It can be appreciated at walking pace in three different ways. The

*The trees of Milford provide an attractive backdrop to this view from the town along Milford Street.*

first is to take the route described in Chapter 5, the length of the Clarendon Way between the centre of Salisbury and Clarendon Palace passing through Milford Hollow and the heart of the old Milford. The second is to walk at right angles to the Clarendon Way on a line from The Avenue (near The Godolphin School) to Weeping Cross that takes you along streets and footpaths right through the heart of the Victorian suburb. And the third is to go to the top of Milford Hill and simply 'poke about' in the many nooks and small lanes, and see what you find, not forgetting to drop down Fowler's Hill to look for the site of the old station, where, if you listen carefully you may hear the cry 'All change at Milford'.

56  No. 96 is at the bottom of Milford Hill. This is because the numbers follow on from those in Milford Street, except that on the south side this system ends at the junction with Fowler's Road, where a new series begins with No. 1.

# Appendices

## 1 Population of Milford, 1801-1911, from censuses

As a tithing of Laverstock and Ford ancient parish:

| | |
|---|---|
| 1801 | 419 |
| 1811 | 394 |
| 1821 | 489 |
| 1831 | 523 |

As a tithing of Salisbury St Martin ancient parish:

| | |
|---|---|
| 1841 | 496 |
| 1851 | 587 |
| 1861 | 631 |
| 1871 | 873 |

As Milford civil parish:

| | | |
|---|---|---|
| 1881 | 2,106 | (of which 1,573 were in the city) |
| 1891 | 3,989 | (of which 3,119 were in the city) |

As two civil parishes (after 1894):

| | | |
|---|---|---|
| 1901 | 3,825 | (Milford Within) |
| | 1,284 | (Milford Without) |
| | 5,109 | |

Another 'Milford' civil parish (the first of that name having been dissolved in 1894) was created in 1904 from parts of Milford Without (pop. 1,470 in 1911) and Stratford-sub-Castle civil parish (pop. 111 in 1911) but it had a short existence, becoming part of Salisbury in 1905.

## 2  Tithe Award 1845

At the time of the Tithe Award and Map of 1845 the tithing of Milford in the parish of Salisbury St Martin contained an estimated quantity of land of 1,356 acres broken down as follows —

| | |
|---|---|
| 867a | arable |
| 162a | water meadows |
| 196a | meadows, pastures and orchards |
| 30a | market gardens and nurseries |
| 1a | woodland |
| 58a | houses and gardens |
| 42a | roads and waste. |

It was formally found that corn, grain and hay tithes were rendered to the Dean and Chapter (who would receive £480 under the award) and all other tithes to the Incumbent of the Rectory of St Martin's (who would receive £165). It was also found that cottage gardens were 'by prescription' absolutely exempt from any render of tithes.

The occupier of Manor House (i.e. Milford Manor) and garden, together with the meadow to the east, the 'close' south of Milford Farm and the stables and coach house on the other side of the road (at the bottom of Milford Hollow) was Isaac Gray; the landowner, himself a lessee of the Lord Farmer [the leaseholder of the manor of Milford], was Wadham Wyndham (of St Edmund's College, the present Council House).

The occupier of the Milford Farm buildings (immediately south of Milford Manor) was Samuel Jones, who farmed all the meadows and fields around the top of Milford Hill and south of Fowler's Hill and Shady Bower.

Moving towards Salisbury, the first prominent house at that time was 'Brome House' (the former 'Blue Post' inn) in Milford Hollow, occupied by John Beckingsale, whose landlord, himself a lessee of the Lord Farmer, was John Sparshott.

After taking the left fork at 'Brome House', one would reach the extensive landholding of Dr Richard Fowler comprising the eastern (or higher) half of the triangle formed by Fowler's Hill, Milford Hill and Rampart/Tollgate Roads. He also owned (subject only to the interest of the Lord Farmer) an area of land between Tollgate Road and Fowler's Hill, most of which would soon be taken for the railway station, and the land on the other side of Tollgate Road that would later be used for the Moore Bros' Boot Factory. Fowler's house, with a number of outbuildings, lay close to Fowler's Hill, but was approached by a long driveway from Tollgate Road, where there was a lodge. The Award does not name the house and in Dr Fowler's lifetime it does not appear to have had a name (though later called 'The Hollies'); in a document of 1859[57] it is called 'Milford Hill House', but no name is given there for Everett's house (see below) so this must have been an error.

The only other large house was 'Milford Hill House' in its extensive grounds. The owner/occupier was Charles Everett of Pinkneys Bank.

The division between city and manor was the line of the medieval rampart. Thus the grounds of St Edmund's College (now the Council House), the home then of the Wyndham family, lay partly in Salisbury and partly in Milford. The same was true of the Greencroft. In both cases leases had been granted of the land in Milford to members of the Wyndham family.

The Godolphin School was still in premises in the Close but would move to Milford Hill very soon (1848). The foundation of Salisbury School (1879) and Cleveland House School (1880) lay in the future. The railway had not yet arrived, though a number of schemes affecting Milford were being actively considered.

---

57   WSRO ref CCBishoprick 165/1 (160671) A Survey and Valuation of the Manors and Estates of Milford and Woodford prepared for the Ecclesiastical Commissioners in connection with the surrender of the manors the following year.

## 3 Extract from *Wiltshire and Somerset Woollen Mills* by Kenneth Rogers, page 256

MILFORD

A fulling mill at Milford was regularly mentioned as part of an estate at Milford Richard which descended in the Milbourne and Faukoner families between 1380 and 1558. It was probably on the site of the present Milford Mill, but no more is known until 1748 when the leasehold of the fulling mill there occupied by William Hussey, clothier was offered for sale. By 1780 the lease belonged to Robert Cooper and between 1786 and 1830 to members of the Sutton family. But the mill was probably underlet to Salisbury clothiers; the tenancy in 1810 for instance was no doubt Samuel Devenish of Milford, clothier. In November 1830 a 'woollen factory' at Milford was destroyed by the Labourers' Revolt. This no doubt marked the end of the trade on this site.

# Bibliography

Boyd Alexander, *England's Wealthiest Son, a study of William Beckford*, Centaur Press (London) 1962.

Charles Arnold-Baker, *Local Council Administration*, Butterworth (London) 2002.

Robert Benson and Henry Hatcher, *Old and New Sarum*, published as part of *The History of Modern Wiltshire* by Sir Richard Colt Hoare Bart., Nichols & Son (London) 1843.

John Chandler, *Endless Street*, The Hobnob Press, (Salisbury) 1983.

J. Cosens *et al.*, *The History of Salisbury's Postal Services, A Report by a Sarum U3A Study Group*, The British Philatelic Trust, 2005.

E. E. Dorling, *Contemporary Biographies, Wilts and Dorset at the opening of the twentieth century*, W. T. Pike & Son, (Brighton) 1906.

M. A. Douglas and C. R. Ash (Eds) *The Godolphin School 1726-1926*, Longmans, Green and Co, (London) 1928.

W. Gaskill, *Wiltshire Leaders*, Queenhithe Printing & Publishing Co. (London) 1906.

J. E. B. Gover *et al*, *Place-names of Wiltshire*, Cambridge University Press 1939.

Charles Haskins, *The Ancient Trade Guilds and Companies of Salisbury*, Bennett Brothers (Salisbury) 1912.

Colin Maggs, *Branch Lines of Wiltshire*, Alan Sutton (Stroud) 2002.

Arthur Maidment, *I Remember, I Remember*, Baverstock Books (Westbury) 1990.

Tim Mowl, *William Beckford, composing for Mozart*, John Murray (London) 1998.

Ruth Newman and Jane Howells, *Salisbury Past*, Phillimore (Chichester) 2001.

John Nicholas & George Reeve, *Main Line to the West*, Irwell Press (Clophill) 2004.

Mike Oakley, *Wiltshire Railway Stations*, The Dovecote Press (Wimborne) 2004

Barbara Reynolds, *The Letters of Dorothy L. Sayers 1899-1936: The Making of a Novelist*, Hodder & Stoughton (London) 1995.

Kenneth Rogers, *Wiltshire and Somerset Woollen Mills*, Pasold Foundation Fund (Edington) 1976.

Royal Commission on Historical Monuments (England), *Salisbury Volume 1* HMSO (London) 1980.

Cecil Woodham Smith, *Florence Nightingale 1820-1910*, Constable (London) 1950.

Frank Stevens, *The Salisbury Museums 1861-1947*, Bennett Brothers (Salisbury) undated.

*Victoria History of the County of Wiltshire*, Volumes 4 and 6 (London).

Wessex Archaeology, *The Upper Thames Valley, the Kennet Valley and the Solent Drainage System*, The Southern Rivers Palaeolithic Project, Report No. 1, (Salisbury) 1993.

Donald C. Whitton, *The Grays of Salisbury, an artist family of nineteenth century England*, Michael Russell (Salisbury) 1979.

### Articles and Documents

Inclosure Award 1800

Tithe Award and Map 1845.

John Andrews and Andrew Dury, *Map of Wiltshire*, 1773.

J.C. Bothams, Plan of the Borough of Salisbury 1860.

M. E. Cunnington, 'Wiltshire in pagan Saxon times', *Wiltshire Archaeological and Natural History magazine*, vol. 46, no. 158 (June 1933), pp. 147-175.

Bruce Eagles, 'The Archaeological Evidence for Settlement in the Fifth to Seventh Centuries AD', in M. Aston and C. Lewis ed. *The Medieval Landscape of Wessex*, Oxbow Monograph 46 1994 pp.13-32.

P. A. Harding and D. R. Bridgland, 'Pleistocene Deposits and Palaeolithic Implements at Godolphin School, Milford Hill, Salisbury', *Wiltshire Archaeological and Natural History Magazine*, Vol. 91 (1998), pp.1-10.

Peter Hart, *Salisbury and Wilton Street Names*, 2001.

John Musty, D. J. Algar and P. F. Ewence, *The Medieval Pottery Kilns at Laverstock, near Salisbury, Wiltshire*, Oxford 1969 (from *Archaeologia* Vol. CII 1969).

T. B. Sands, 'The Railways of Salisbury – 1', *Railway Magazine* (August 1961).

Brian Tippett, 'E. M. Forster in Wiltshire: the making of *The Longest Journey*', *The Hatcher Review* vol. 5, no.47 (1999), pp. 6-21.

# Index

Numbers in **bold** refer to captions of illustrations

Æthelwulf, 8fn

Alderbury, hundred of, 9

'Arnon Bridge', 23-24, **24**

Atkins, Samuel, 58, 59

Avon, River, 8, 13

Barber, Nathaniel, 30, **30**, 61

Bath, Fred, 61, 64

Beckford, William, 20, **20**, 53-54, **54, 55**

Bishopsdown Farm, 17, 18-19

Bishopsdown, 14, 36

Bourne, River, 5, 8, 10, 11, 15

Brome House, 22, **22**, 69

Building materials, 66

Chafyn Grove School, 25, 28-29, **29**, 48fn, 64-65

Cholera outbreak of 1849, 32, 46

Clarendon, 8, 9, 37

Clarendon Way, 36

Cleveland School, 29-30, **30**

Cow Lane, 54

Cripps, William, 59, 62

Domesday Book, 12, 14, 15

Douglas, Mary, 59

Dust Hole/ Railway Inn, 46, **46**

Ecclesiastical Commission, 26, 28

Elm Grove Estate, 26

Everett, Charles, 55

Fawcett, Sarah M, 48, 58, **58**

Fielding, Henry, 52-53

Forster, E.M., 57

Fowler, Dr Richard, 25, 32, 44, 54-55, 69

Fowler's Hill, 25, 26, 38

Fowler's Road, 26

Gerrish, Richard, 30, 59, **59**

Godolphin School, 25, 29, 39, 46-51, 54, 58, 63, 65-66

Greencroft (The), 69

Hamilton, Duke of, 26, 45

Higher Terrace Gravel, **6**, 33

Holmleigh, 49, 57

Kelsey House, 28, 64

Laverstock, 5, 14, 21, 68

Laverstock pottery industry, 15-16

Little Manor, **18**, 21-22

Lovibond, Joseph, 50

Manchester, 42, 43

Market Place, Salisbury, 36

Milford (origin of name), 5

Milford, Lord Farmer of (meaning), 20

Milford, Manor of, 8, 17

Milford, tithing of, 10,69

Milford Bridge, 5, 7, 16, 60

Milford Cottage, 63

Milford Episcopi, 6, 7, 9, 14, 15

Milford Farm, 18

Milford Grove, 46-47

Milford Hall Hotel, 8

Milford Hill House, 25, 31, 55-56, 62, 69

Milford Hill, meaning of, 10fn

Milford Hollow, 36-40, 43

Milford Manor Gardens, 21, 30

Milford Manor, 19, **19**, 21, 30, 59, 60, 61

Milford Pichard, 7, 9, 14, 15

Milford Preservation Group, 11

Milford Railway Station, 41-45

Milford Richard, 7, 9, 14, 15

Milford Street, 37, 67, **67**

Milford Villa (see 'Milford Grove')

Milford Ward, 11

Milford Within, parish of, 10, 11, 68

Milford Without, parish of,

10, 11, 68

Modern School (see 'Cleveland School')

Moore, James & William, 56

Mount, The, 58, 66

Mumworth, 14

Nelson, Earl, 25fn, 58

Newlands, 58, 64, **65**

Nightingale, Florence, 55

Old Coach House, 62, **63**

Old House (The), (see 'Newlands')

Palaeontology, 12, 14, **14**, 33-34

Pepper, George, 57

Petersfinger Road, 10, 60

Pillar boxes, 66-67

Pinckney, William, 55-56, **56**, 58

Population figures, 68

Punch Bowl, 22-23

Railway Inn/Dust Hole, 46, **46**

Rose Villa, 40, 49

Rougemont, 58

St Edmund's College, 26, 69

St Martin, parish of, 8, **8**, 68

St Martin's Primary School, 35

St Probus School, 63

Saxon finds, 14

Sayers, Dorothy L., 25fn, 49-50

Shady Bower, 22, 40, 43, 44, 47, **62**

Swayne, Bennet, 53, **53**

Tintometer (The) Ltd, 45, 50

Tithe Award & Map, 10, **26**, 68-69

Underditch, hundred of, 9

Waterloo Flour Mills, 45

Woollen mill, 16, 21, 69-70

Young, Edwin, 39

Youth Hostel (see 'Milford Hill House')